# TRAVELLERS

# NORTHERN
# ITALY

By
**LARA DUNSTON & TERRY CARTER**

**Written by Lara Dunston & Terry Carter**
Original photography by Terry Carter

**Published by Thomas Cook Publishing**
A division of Thomas Cook Tour Operations Limited
Company registration no. 3772199 England
The Thomas Cook Business Park, Unit 9, Coningsby Road,
Peterborough PE3 8SB, United Kingdom
Email: books@thomascook.com, Tel: + 44 (0) 1733 416477
www.thomascookpublishing.com

**Produced by Cambridge Publishing Management Limited**
Burr Elm Court, Main Street, Caldecote CB23 7NU

ISBN: 978-1-84848-096-4

© 2009 Thomas Cook Publishing
Text © Thomas Cook Publishing
Maps © Thomas Cook Publishing/PCGraphics (UK) Limited

Series Editor: Maisie Fitzpatrick
Production/DTP: Steven Collins

Printed and bound in Italy by Printer Trento

Cover photography: Front L–R: © Cogoli Franco/4CR; © CW Images/Alamy;
© Giovanni Simeone/4CR
Back: © Giovanni Simeone/4CR

# Contents

# Introduction

*Northern Italy is a sensory experience and a sophisticated one; fine art, music, cuisine, wine, natural beauty and some of the most beautiful objects created by man. Northern Italy is where Italy reveals itself as a multi-layered experience – beyond the stereotypes of flashy red sports cars, chic fashion and spaghetti Bolognese. Despite the fact that it's the home of all three!*

No other region of Italy, or for that matter Europe, has the variety of vistas and experiences that can match that of Northern Italy: from museums brimming with great works of art and cathedrals where frescoes look like they could come to life, to mountain ranges that challenge visitors to ski down and climb up them and shady park benches that entice you to take in the reflections of a beautiful lake.

Every meal in Northern Italy is a treat, from the simplest *osteria* (small local eatery) to Michelin-starred houses of haute cuisine. There is always something new to try as each area has its own regional specialities and its own matching wines. But what makes the North so unique is that there are subtle and not so subtle differences between (and even within) each region, in how locals play out their lives.

For example, Milan might be the engine room of Italy's economy, but it's no buttoned-down city. It's the home of Italian fashion, the ritual of the after-work *aperitivo* or cocktail hour, brilliant art by Leonardo da Vinci and the Renaissance masters, and one of the most beautiful Gothic cathedrals in the world. As the seasons change, so do recreational habits. In summer the surrounding lakes such as Lago di Como beckon, while in winter the opera season begins and the Alps await for a weekend of skiing.

While Milan is considered the North's most serious city, Venice is easily the most romantic. The gondolier (oarsman) ducking under one of the city's 409 bridges as he takes tourists on a tour through the maze-like canals might be one of the most overexposed travel images on the planet, but it's still one of the most compelling when seen with your own eyes.

Almost matching Venice for romance is the city of Verona, the setting of Shakespeare's *Romeo and Juliet* and home to one of the most magnificent Roman amphitheatres in the world, where the summer opera season is an open-air delight. On the coast, Portofino is the choice for the jet set who dive off the back of their sleek white yachts, before feasting on seafood and champagne.

However, while taking in these classic experiences, you soon discover that there is a pattern to life, something that unifies these diverse encounters – Northern Italians simply know how to live. From the ritual of the afternoon *passagietta* (promenade) to lingering over a multi-course meal, work, even in the industrious North, is only a part of life – it doesn't define it. Family is most important. Friends are important. And celebrating the richness of art, music, cuisine and wine is important. When you travel through Northern Italy, the locals just want you to do the same.

Introduction

A gondola cruise along the Grand Canal is a great introduction to Venice

# The land

*Northern Italy is a study in contrasts, from the flat uniformity of the land around Milan, to the languid lakes and the spectacular mountains that form the border to its neighbours. While these natural barriers should have made the region easy to defend, the richness of the soil and the beauty of the surrounds have made it a magnet for invaders and migrants who tackled the region on foot, on horseback and even on the backs of elephants.*

The Alps separate Italy from neighbouring France, Switzerland, Austria and Slovenia. Indeed, much of Italy is mountainous and rugged – more than one third has an elevation of over 700m (2,300ft) – with the Apennines running the length of the Italian 'boot' all the way down to the tip

Summer at Cannobio, Lago Maggiore

in Calabria. The main relief in Italy, in the form of plains, is in the north, in the triangular shaped area of the Po Valley, which runs around 600km (373 miles) in an east-west direction.

The Alps can be roughly divided into three groups. The western Alps run north-south along the Swiss and French border from Aosta to the sea near Monaco. This group includes Gran Paradiso, the highest peak in Italy at 4,061m (13,323ft). The central Alps, running west-east from the western Alps, ending at the Brenner Pass, are considered the home of modern mountaineering and include peaks such as Mont Blanc, the Matterhorn and Monte Rosa. The eastern Alps run from the Brenner Pass to Trieste and include the Dolomites and the famous ski resort of Cortina d'Ampezzo.

Oak, olive and cypress trees thrive at the foothills of the Alps, while higher up, beech gives way to spruce and then to juniper. While wildlife in Italy isn't

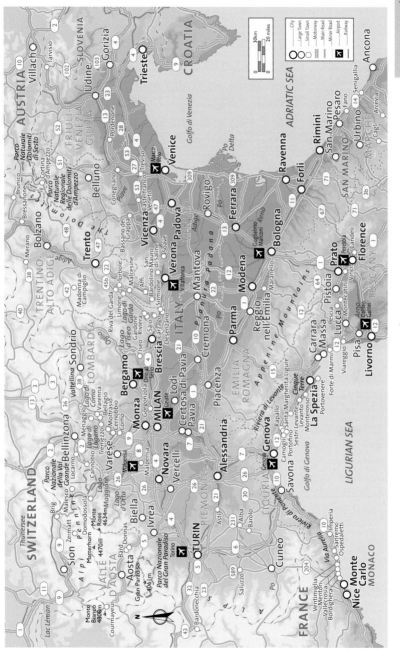

The Cinque Terre coastline at Corniglia

all that abundant, the Alps are home to ibex and deer, although the protected brown bear is now rare. Alpine birds, however, are more common, with black grouse and golden eagle often spotted.

Below the central and eastern Alps lie the great lakes of Northern Italy, the largest of which are Garda, Maggiore, Como, Iseo and Lugano, from largest to smallest. Glaciers running through the valleys of the Alpine foothills formed these lakes, which today have a sub-Mediterranean climate.

South from this is the Po River (running west-east), Italy's longest at 645km (400 miles), with tributaries running through the region and passing through or near Turin, Asti, Milan, Brescia and Verona, eventually running into the Adriatic Sea. The Po Valley is actually a former gulf, filled in by silt running down from the Alps,

and is a geologically recent feature. The southern part of the Po is most suited to agriculture; however, the seasons can bring frost and hailstorms, playing havoc with the area's grain crops.

The people of these regions see themselves as more serious and hard-working than those in the South, who have a more 'take-it-as-it-comes' attitude, which is generally in line with the Italian stereotype. While these might be generalisations, Milan *is* the 'engine room' of Italian industry and the economy. The contrasts are vivid within the region too, especially when, say, a Milanese banker goes to the mountains on a ski trip and meets local Italians who might speak German as a first language, live off the land and eat dishes not found in Milan.

The constant migration, the influence of passing armies, the proximity to the distinctly different cultures of neighbouring countries and the isolation of the rugged Alps, all contribute to making this part of Italy less classically 'Italian' than you would perhaps expect. One of the reasons for this is that the Italians who emigrated to other countries such as Argentina, Australia and the United States mostly came from the poor southern regions of the country, and the Italian stereotype presented in the media and on film is generally one from Southern Italy.

The unique cultures and linguistic minorities of the North are strongly protected in Valle d'Aosta, Friuli-Venezia Giulia and Trentino-Alto Adige, where there is little sign that these cultures will wane. You'll find that many people here are happily trilingual, speaking whatever language will take the conversation further. These areas make Northern Italy unique, and the lack of migration to these more remote regions from immigrants streaming into Italy doesn't look like this will be changing anytime soon.

The land

The riverside in Verona

# History

| | |
|---|---|
| **Around 3300 BC** | Era of the 'iceman', Ötzi (now on display in Bolzano, *see p112*). |
| **3000 BC** | Northern lakes region inhabited by prehistoric peoples who lived in caves at Valpolicella, near Verona, and around Lago Iseo. |
| **5th–4th centuries BC** | Ligurians (of whom little is known) inhabit the Po Valley. |
| **280 BC** | Roman legions arrive in the Po Valley and soon rule all of the region later known as Italy. |
| **222 BC** | Romans occupy Mediolanum (ancient Milan). |
| **218–200 BC** | Second Punic War, Hannibal crosses the Alps. The Celts push the Romans south of the Po. Romans regain Mediolanum. |
| **89 BC** | Verona and Brescia become full Roman colonies. |
| **15 BC** | Mediolanum is made the capital of the Roman 11th region. |
| **AD 313** | Edict of Milan – Emperor Constantine recognises Christianity. |
| **410** | Beginning of Visigoth invasions from the north. They sack Rome. |
| **452–93** | Germanic Ostrogoths seize control. Attila the Hun sacks Milan. |
| **568–71** | Lombards and other Germanic tribes conquer the North, some convert to Christianity. |
| **774** | The Frankish King, Charlemagne, defeats Lombards and is made King of the Lombards. |
| **1155** | Frederick Barbarossa is crowned Emperor of the Holy Roman Empire. |
| **1162** | Barbarossa lays siege to Milan. |
| **1277** | Visconti rule of Milan begins. |
| **1347–50** | The 'Black Death' plague reaches Venice. Italy loses one third of its population. |

| | | | |
|---|---|---|---|
| **1450** | Venice controls most of the eastern Mediterranean. | **1936** | Hitler and Mussolini form a pact called The Axis. |
| **1499** | The Sforza, who took over after Visconti rule, cede Milan to France. | **1940** | Italy joins World War II as a German ally. |
| **1559** | Spain controls Milan. | **1943** | Mussolini is deposed and sets up a puppet state at Salò on Lago di Garda. |
| **1706** | The Austrians claim Milan from Spain. | **1944** | Italy joins the Allies; Italian partisans battle Nazis in occupied areas. |
| **1805** | Napoleon is crowned King of Italy. | **1945** | Mussolini is caught at Lago di Como and killed in Guilino di Mezzegra. |
| **1815** | Austria regains Lombardia. | **1946** | Vittorio Emanuele III abdicates. The Republic of Italy is declared. |
| **1831** | The Young Italy movement is founded and begins resistance to Austria. | **1957** | Italy joins the European Economic Community. |
| **1848** | Austrians win the First War of Italian Independence. | **1970–85** | Red Brigades terrorise Milan and other cities. |
| **1858** | Second War of Italian Independence. The battle of Solferino leads to the founding of the Red Cross and Geneva Conventions. | **1996** | Arsonists destroy Venice's La Fenice opera house. |
| **1861** | Vittorio Emanuele II is crowned King of Italy. | **2002** | Italy adopts the euro. |
| **1870** | The unification of the Kingdom of Italy is completed. | **2006** | Winter Olympics in Turin. Prime Minister Berlusconi is replaced by Romano Prodi. |
| **1915** | Italy joins the Allies against Germany in World War I. | **2008** | Berlusconi regains office with a new political party. |

# Politics

*Italy is a Parliamentary Republic with two legislative Houses, a chamber of deputies and a senate, working under a constitution adopted in 1948 after the monarchy was abolished in 1946. It has a multi-party system and executive power is exercised by a Council of Ministers, led by a prime minister. Both Houses of Parliament, as well as regional representatives, elect a president for a seven-year term. The president assumes much of the role of a head of state and is a point of connection between the branches of power.*

As for Italy's performance as a Parliamentary Republic, there are two sides to the coin. Italians have democratic rights – it's just that they have to practise them so often! Since 1948 there have been 62 governments, and even after changes to the system after the dawn of the 'Second Republic'

Alessandro Manzoni stirred political activism with his writing

in 1992 (essentially to combat political paralysis and corruption), political stability is still not forthcoming. For Italians, change is the only constant – apart from Milan's political stalwart Silvio Berlusconi's frequent appearance as Prime Minister (1994–1995, 2001–2006, 2008–).

Italy is divided into 20 regions whose governments have administrative powers. These regions are further broken down into provinces and municipalities (*comuni*). For instance, the Emilia Romagna region is divided into nine provinces: Bologna (the capital), Ferrara, Forlì-Cesena, Modena, Parma, Piacenza, Ravenna, Reggio Emilia and Rimini. Five of the regions of Italy have special autonomous capacity, allowing them to enact legislation relating to local matters, particularly to do with cultural minorities. They are Valle d'Aosta, Friuli-Venezia Giulia and Trentino-Alto Adige, and the islands of Sardinia and Sicily.

Local government building in Genova

The elephant in the room of Northern Italian politics is the *Lega Nord per l'Indipendenza della Padania* or Northern League. Formed in 1991, it has been advocating fiscal federalism and greater regional autonomy that has sometimes drifted into an acknowledgement that secession from greater Italy is a long-term goal, calling the region 'Pandania'. One of the interesting things about the party is that it embraces anyone who wants autonomy and federalism, so it has members from the far left to the far right of the political spectrum. As idealistic as that sounds, the party has been controversial, with charges of racism and perceived endorsement of violence against immigrants under the guise of preserving Northern Italian culture.

The eternally opportunistic Silvio Berlusconi has needed the support of the Northern League to form governments, so since the 2008 election the party has four ministers in Berlusconi's government, resulting in a gain of around 8.5 per cent of the national vote. In order to get back into power, Berlusconi formed a new party combining his centre-right *Forza Italia* party with the right-wing National Alliance party. The ploy proved successful, with the party receiving a solid majority and the story of this most colourful character starting a new chapter – with Berlusconi at 71 years of age.

# Culture

*Italy arguably boasts Europe's richest culture, with countless museums displaying masterpieces of Italian and international fine art and objects, splendid opera houses that host some of the finest opera companies and orchestras in the world, and buildings that are testaments to some of the world's great architectural movements, from the Palladian palaces in the Veneto to the modernism of Milan.*

## Music

Oddly enough, it was Milan's bishop, Saint Ambrose, who initiated the first notable music coming out of Milan. His Ambrosian chants, dating from around AD 374, became the Ambrosian Rites, still practised today. Cremona is the home of the modern stringed instrument, and the Cremonese composer Claudio Monteverdi (*c*.1567–1643) is credited with initiating the move from the Renaissance to the Baroque. His opera *L'Orfeo* is one of the earliest-known pieces of this art form and is still performed today. Around this time in Venice, the Venetian School was in full swing, a creative movement that was also ushering in the Baroque, with its wide influence spreading across Europe.

In the early 1800s, a young man from the Po Valley, whose application to Milan's prestigious conservatoire was rejected, went on to become one of the most influential opera composers of the 19th century. Giuseppe Verdi (1813–1901) became a fixture at Milan's La Scala – the centre of the opera universe in Italy, writing famous operas such as *Rigoletto* (1851), *La Traviata* (1853), *Don Carlos* (1867) and *Aida* (1871), as well as his *Requiem Mass* (1874). It was *Aida* that inspired a young Giacomo Puccini (1858–1924) to leave Tuscany and study in Milan. His operas, *La Bohème* (1896), *Tosca* (1900), *Madama Butterfly* (1904) and the sadly unfinished *Turandot*, have transcended the opera world and are part of popular culture, with opera singer Luciano Pavarotti's version of *Nessun Dorma* (None Shall Sleep Tonight) from *Turandot* becoming an unexpected top ten hit.

## Fine art

When one thinks of art in Northern Italy, clearly the star of the show is Leonardo da Vinci's *The Last Supper* in the convent of Santa Maria delle Grazie in Milan. The prototypical polymath or Renaissance man, da Vinci

A concert at the Palazzo Marino in Milan

(1452–1519) came to Milan to paint the church mural in 1495, finishing the work in 1498, and this painting is often said to be the starting point of the High Renaissance. While the painting is a must-see, Milan's Pinacoteca di Brera has the most breathtaking art collection in Northern Italy.

Giotto (1266–1337) was a Lombard artist whose magnum opus is the decoration of the Scrovegni Chapel in Padua. Regarded as the father of modern painting, he broke away from Byzantine forms, and was a great influence on the religious frescoes by Giovanni da Milano (1346–69). Andrea Mantegna (1430–1506) was a dominant figure in the 15th-century Milanese School. Mantegna's masterpiece, *The Dead Christ*, is a highlight of the Pinacoteca di Brera. Also influential was Milanese painter Michelangelo

Merisi di Caravaggio (1573–1610) whose new naturalism relied on using models from the street. In Venice, Giovanni Bellini (c.1430–1516) was the best known of a family of Venetian painters working during the early Renaissance and notable for his sumptuous *Virgin and Child* paintings. Later in Venice, the artist known as Canaletto (1697–1768) became renowned for wonderful landscapes of the waterways of his city.

### Fashion

While today Milan is without doubt one of the world's great fashion capitals, it wasn't until the 1950s that many haute-couture houses, such as Gucci, moved to Milan from Florence. The biannual fashion shows came too, and while New York's and Paris's are the most important women's fashion shows of the year, Milan is the undisputed centre for men's fashion. While Prada had been in Milan since 1913, perhaps the biggest impact on the fashion scene was Giorgio Armani's 1982 *Prêt-à-porter* (ready-to-wear) collection, which was actually affordable – not to mention attractive. This is a key point of Milan fashion. It usually features generally practical classicists such as Prada, Gucci and Valentino who make clothes with a timeless quality about them. Many of the fashion houses have also moved into home décor, furniture

Turin, World Design Capital for 2008

and hotels, Armani being the most successful practitioner in this expansion into other fields.

## Design

Northern Italy is *the* home of Italian design. Both Milan and Turin were heavily influential in the post World War II era with designs that were sleek and sensual and yet had life, defining Italian style. In Milan, Gio Ponti (1891–1979), an architect, industrial designer and influential design publisher, was the linchpin of the movement. Many of these designs from the second half of the 20th century now adorn museums all over the world. An influential designer who worked for Ponti was Carlo Mollino, who also started as an architect before moving into other fields. His Arabesque table of glass and oak, a classic and rare piece by Mollino, famously sold for $3.8 million at a Christie's auction in 2005. The 1980s saw the playful designs of kitchenware company Alessi become extraordinarily popular.

Industrial design in Turin has been a little more serious. Olivetti, the typewriter company, had brilliant designers in Mario Bellini, making calculators that are now behind glass in museums, while Ettore Sottsass designed typewriters that are still much sought-after. But it was the independent car design firms that generated the most excitement. Giorgetto Giugiaro (Italdesign-

Giugiaro) and Battista 'Pinin' Farina (Pininfarina) created some of the most breathtaking car designs for Ferrari and Alfa Romeo and are still active today.

## Cinema

While the first screenings of films occurred in Milan in 1896, it wasn't until Turin's production studios blossomed in the early 20th century that Northern Italy became obsessed with cinema, with the first blockbuster being *Cabiria* (1914). While Mussolini nationalised cinema production in the 1930s, it was in the post-war period that Milan's great director, the Marxist Luchino Visconti (1906–76), came to prominence. Working in the neo-realistic style, which favoured stories set amongst the working classes, and with low budgets and non-professional actors, Visconti's *Rocco e i suoi fratelli* (Rocco and His Brothers, 1960), a tragic tale of southerners who come to Milan to look for work, is one of the most popular films of that era. *Miracolo a Milano* (Miracle in Milan, 1951), directed by Vittorio De Sica, was another film set in Milan that won the Grand Prize at the Cannes Film Festival for its wonderful satire. While the Venice Film Festival is still a prestigious event these days, the appeal of Italian film in other markets is limited.

## Literature

Poetry was always a form of literary expression in Italy, and arguably its greatest proponent was Francesco

Only an Italian could pull off wearing a three-piece suit while riding a scooter!

Petrarca (1304–74). His poems, addressed to an idealised love named Laura, were highly influential in the Renaissance period. Another poet, Alessandro Manzoni (1785–1873), wrote what is considered the Italian masterpiece, the novel *I Promessi Sposi* (The Betrothed). Set in 17th-century Milan, the novel was treated as a nationalistic clarion call when released in the 1840s. Of contemporary authors, none looms larger than Milan-based intellectual Umberto Eco (1932–). He is best known for his novels *Il Nome della Rosa* (The Name of the Rose, 1980) and *Il Pendolo di Foucault* (Foucault's Pendulum, 1988).

# Festivals and events

*From opera in Verona's breathtaking Roman arena, to Venice's colourful Carnevale and to celebrations of music, food, wine and anything else they can think of, Northern Italy loves festivities. Travellers should definitely try to align their visit with a festival, as it's a great way to interact with the locals – who really know how to enjoy themselves!*

## January

**Mezzanotte di Fiaba** News Year's Eve. Fireworks at Riva del Garda.
**Corteo dei Re Magi** Epiphany day, 6 January: 'Wise Men Processional' in Milan.
**Foire de Saint Ours** Handicrafts festival at Aosta.
**Carnevale di Verona** Parades, bands, fashion and costumes in Verona.

## February

**Carnevale Ambrosiano** Milan's Carnival.
**Carnevale** Re-creation of the 18th-century Venetian Republic, with decorative costumes and parties in Venice.
**Festival della canzone Italiana (Festival of Italian Popular Song)** Three-day festival of pop in Sanremo, Italian Riviera.

## March

**Milano Internazionale Antiquariato** Renowned international antique show in Milan.

## April

**Liberazione (Liberation Day)** Parades and celebrations on 25 April.
**Salone Internazionale del Mobile** Europe's largest furniture fair in Milan.

## May

**Antica Fiera dei Mangiari** Medieval fair with a focus on food and local produce in Mantova.
**Festa del Caroccio** Costumed parade commemorating the 1176 battle in Legnano.
**Medieval White Wine Festival** in Soave.
**Le Piazze dei Sapori** 'Square of Flavours', several-day festival of local produce and wines in Verona.

## June

**Festa del Naviglio** Ten days of concerts, art, sports, cooking and an antique market in Milan.
**Festival of San Giovanni** Fireworks at Isola Comacina on Lake Como.
**Garda Jazz Festival** A couple of weeks of great jazz at Riva del Garda.

Milano d'Estate Varied musical concerts in Parco Sempione in Milan, June–August.

Opera Festival Performances at the Arena in Verona, June–August.

La Biennale de Venezia Modern Art exhibition on even years, Venice.

Shakespearean Festival Celebrating the Bard, June–September, Verona.

## July

Notturni in Villa Concerts in city villas, Milan.

Verona Vinorum Wine festival, Verona.

Festival Latino Americano Two months of Latin American culture (performances, food etc) in Milan, July–August.

Festa del Redentore Feast of the Redeemer, floating fiesta with fireworks, Venice.

## August

Ferragosto Feast of the Assumption throughout the region, public holiday, various celebrations – processions, church services, feasts.

Festival del Film di Locarno Ten days of open-air film screenings, Locarno.

Rustico Medioevo Medieval dance and folklore on the Canale di Tenno, Riva del Garda.

Venice International Film Festival

Rossini Opera Festival Celebrates the composer's operas, Pesaro.

## September

Festival Milano Contemporary music, dance, theatre in Milan, September–October.

Festa dell'Uva Grape festival, Soave.

Italian Formula One Grand Prix, Monza.

Regatta Storica Sees the Grand Canal in Venice packed with gondolas.

## October

Bardolino Wine Festival, Bardolino.

Chestnut Festival Harvest festivities and opportunities to try chestnuts in different recipes, San Mauro di Saline, Verona Province.

Milano International Film Festival, Milan.

Sagra del Tartufo Celebrating the beginning of the truffle season, Alba. Opportunities to try truffles – they feature on menus throughout town.

Salone del Gusto (Slow Food Festival) Celebrates traditional cooking, Turin.

## November

Tutti Santi All Saints' Day, throughout the region.

Festa della Salute, Venice (massive religious festival).

Merano Wine Festival & Culinaria Focuses on excellent local food and wine, Merano.

## December

Feast of Sant'Ambrogio 7 December, throughout the region, public holiday.

La Scala Season Opening 7 December, Milan.

Festa del Immacolata 8 December, throughout the region, public holiday.

Stalls of Santa Lucia Christmas fair in Piazza Bra, Verona.

# Highlights

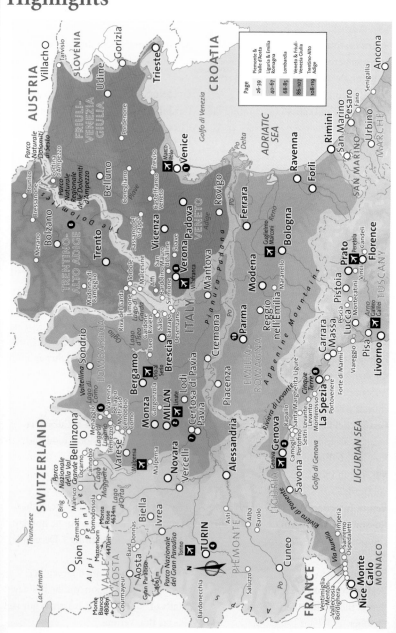

| Page | |
|------|-----|
| 26–39 | Piemonte & Valle d'Aosta |
| 40–67 | Liguria & Emilia Romagna |
| 68–85 | Lombardia |
| 86–107 | Veneto & Friuli-Venezia Giulia |
| 108–119 | Trentino-Alto Adige |

**1 Venice** The world's most spellbinding city may not be so tranquil anymore but *La Serenissima* ('the most serene') still works her magic, despite the crowds (*see pp87–97*).

**2 Milan's Duomo** Boasting 3,500 statues, 135 spires, 52 pillars and a gold *Madonnina*, Milan's Gothic cathedral is captivating. Walk among the rooftop angels for complete bewitchment (*see p71*).

**3 Genova** Marvel at the granite and marble-striped churches before getting lost in the skinny cobblestone streets of the maze-like medieval centre at this cosmopolitan port city (*see pp42–7*).

**4 Turin** With its wide boulevards, graceful squares and grand arcades, Italy's design capital must be the country's most elegant city (*see pp27–33*).

**5 Lago di Como** Explore Lake Como's enchanting villages with their vine-covered villas and rose-filled gardens (*see pp78–81*).

**6 Dolomite Mountains** Meander through the heart of this dramatic mountain range of craggy grey pinnacles, fairytale castles and Alpine villages – on foot, skis or wheels (*see pp114–15 & 118–19*).

**7 Certosa di Pavia** Be astonished at the grandeur and extravagance of this Renaissance Carthusian monastery, then reflect upon the riches as you stroll the serene cloistered garden (*see p85*).

**8 Verona's Old Town** This romantic riverside city boasts beautiful frescoed buildings, splendid churches and squares, a colossal crenellated castle, and ancient Roman arena (*see pp103–5*).

**9 Cinque Terre coastline** For the most dramatic sea and mountain vistas, drive or walk between these entrancing pastel-coloured villages on the lush Ligurian coast (*see pp54–7*).

**10 Parma's gastronomic delights** Gastronomes will be in food heaven at Parma, home to such gourmet delights as *prosciutto crudo* and *Parmigiano Reggiano*, and some of Italy's tastiest cuisine (*see pp62–3*).

Vernazza, Cinque Terre

# Suggested itineraries

Stylish, sophisticated and seductive, and oozing history and culture from every cobblestone street, Northern Italy may contain the country's most industrialised regions but it also boasts the most compelling sights with enough chic cities, enchanting lakes, mountain resorts and charming villages to occupy you for a lifetime. Whether you're doing a weekend city-break in modish Milan or elegant Turin or a grand tour of the whole north, you'll never be bored.

## Long weekend

For a leisurely long weekend on the lakes, fly into Milan or Bergamo airport, pick up a hire car and begin

A ferry plies Lake Como

your exploration with the most breathtakingly beautiful expanse of water, Lago di Como. Base yourself at one of the big old lakeside piles and spend a day or two doing a circuit of the lake, calling in to Como, Bellagio, Menaggio and Varenna. Drive west and spend another couple of days exploring Lago d'Orta and Lago Maggiore, making sure not to miss the sweet villages of Orta San Giulio and grand Verbania, and one of the most alluring lakeside villages of all, Cannobio.

## One week

A one-week gourmet food and wine tour of Northern Italy will give you a taste of the many gastronomic delights of this wonderful part of Italy. Focus on the regions of Emilia-Romagna and Lombardia. Emilia-Romagna is home to Parmesan cheese, cured meats, pastas such as fettucini, tortellini and tortelli, and balsamic vinegar. It boasts several excellent museums of food offering tours and tastings. In Emilia-Romagna, spend a night each in Parma, Modena and Bologna, home to some of Italy's best *trattorie* serving up hearty pastas and local specialities – horse meat is a favourite! Parma is the place to head to a *salumeria* to buy *prosciutto crudo* (raw cured ham) and aged *Parmigiano Reggiano* (parmesan cheese), or go direct to the source at Reggio Emilia, the birthplace of the crumbly aged

Statue of Ferdinando di Savoia in Turin

cheese. In Modena visit the world's oldest delicatessen, *Salumeria Giusti*, dating to 1605. Modena is where to buy the world's best aged balsamic vinegar, *Aceto Balsamico Tradizionale di Modena*. In Bologna, visit the narrow market lanes off the main square and let your nose lead you to the mouthwatering aromas wafting from the stores selling delicious cheeses, meats and the local speciality, *mortadella* sausage. Bologna is home to *ragù*, the slow-cooked, minced pasta sauce known as *Bolognese* in some parts of the world. In Lombardia, enjoy inventive contemporary cuisine with a long, leisurely tasting menu at one of the many Michelin-starred restaurants on one of the lakes or in Milan. Wine buffs can match their local specialities with regional wines. Try sparkling

Lambrusco in Modena and a serious Colli di Parma in Parma, and don't miss a robust Sangiovese or light Trebbiano di Romagna. Your last stop should be Peck in Milan, a temple to all things delectable to buy some of these treats to take home.

Alternatively, you could spend a week appreciating the wonderful array of great art and architecture of Northern Italy. If you want to cram in as much as possible, do a tour of the region's fine cities with three days in Venice, two days in Milan and a day each in Genova and Turin, all of which boast outstanding art museums, superlative works of art, and architectural gems. Venice is home to the Gallerie dell'Accademia and Peggy Guggenheim Collection, both world-class art museums. Piazza San Marco (which

A detail from the façade of Milan's Duomo

Napoleon called 'the world's most beautiful drawing room') is the address of two of Italy's finest buildings, Basilica di San Marco and Palazzo Ducale. Then there's the gamut of architecture on Grand Canal, from Gothic (Ca' Foscari, Ca' d'Oro) and Renaissance (Palazzo Vendramin-Calergi, San Giorgio Maggiore) to Baroque (Ca' Rezzonico, Santa Maria di Nazareth and San Stae). Milan has the brilliant Pinacoteca di Brera, Pinacoteca Ambrosiana and the Museo Poldi-Pezzoli, and Leonardo da Vinci's *Il Cenacola* (The Last Supper) at Santa Maria delle Grazie church. In Turin, visit the Galleria Sabauda (home to the vast Savoy art collections) and Museo d'Arte Antica (with over 30,000 art pieces from the Middle Ages), and in Genova, Palazzo Reale and Galleria Nazionale. Milan, Turin and Genova also boast beautiful cathedrals, churches, palaces and castles.

## Two weeks

With two weeks to spare, you can sample the best Northern Italy has to offer by train or car, beginning and ending in Milan or Venice. Spend a couple of days each in the cities of Milan, Venice, Turin and Genova, easily Northern Italy's most engaging cities, with overnight stops in some of the North's most compelling towns in between, such as Bergamo, Verona, Parma, Modena and Bologna. Alternatively, you could break up your busy city stays with some down time in the countryside, by hiring a car for a few days for a drive through the pristine Dolomites (easily accessible from Verona), the tranquil lakes (from Milan for Lago di Como, Maggiore and d'Orta, and from Verona for Garda and Iseo), the ruggedly beautiful Cinque Terre (a short drive or train ride from Genova), and enchanting Valle d'Aosta (close to Turin).

## Longer

In one month you can do a 'grand tour' of the whole of Northern Italy, spending a couple of days in the major cities and single nights in towns and villages. From Milan, head for Como and spend some time exploring the lakes. Drive down to Turin and to Genova via Asti.

Next stop should be Camiglio, then Cinque Terre. Head up to the Emilia-Romagna towns of Parma, Modena and Bologna, and from here Ravenna and Ferrara are easy drives away. Tackle Venice next; parking is expensive and a nightmare, so make advance arrangements with your hotel. From Venice, you could visit Trieste and Udine, then Cortina d'Ampezzo, Bolzano, Trento, Verona and Bergamo, before returning to Milan. If that pace is too fast for you, cross some cities out and instead spend more time relaxing at the lakes, five days hiking between the Cinque Terre villages, and a few days walking or skiing in the Dolomite Mountains.

For something different, you could drive to San Remo and from there cross the border to France and Monaco for a day.

Corniglia, one of the Cinque Terre villages

# Piemonte and Valle d'Aosta

Piemonte *means foothill, an apt name considering most of its cities and towns are set in lovely undulating hills and lush valleys surrounded by majestic mountains. It is one of the most beautiful parts of Italy, with Turin exactly in the middle of the Piemonte-Valle d'Aosta region, the gorgeous Langhe wine region south of the city and the charming towns of Aosta, Alba, Asti and Barolo, while north is the semi-autonomous bilingual Valle d'Aosta.*

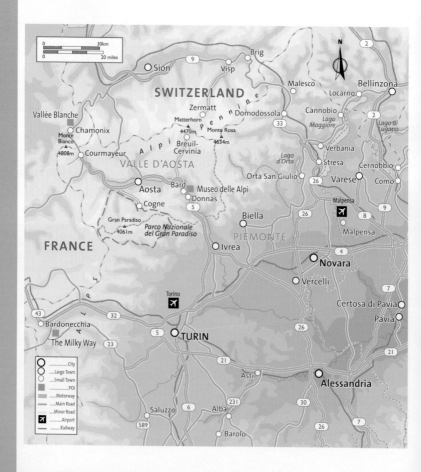

The valleys of the Valle d'Aosta are carved by steep gorges and dotted with fairytale hilltop castles, and the drive from Turin to Aosta on the S5 is a jaw-dropping delight. A must-stop on the way is the cutting-edge Museo delle Alpi (Museum of the Alps) at the rebuilt Forte di Bard between Bard and Donnas. Aosta makes a great base for exploring the surrounding valleys and mountains, the Parco Nazionale del Gran Paradiso (National Park of Gran Paradiso), Monte Bianco (Mont Blanc) and the ski resorts of the Alps, such as Courmayeur and Breuil-Cervinia.

## Turin

With street after street of splendid buildings, grand arcades, leafy tree-lined boulevards, lovely sunny squares and manicured lawns, Turin is without a doubt Italy's most elegant city.

Founded as a Roman garrison town and base for the troops in Gaul, it was known as Augusta Taurinorum. From the Middle Ages through to the mid-16th century, Turin was at times occupied by the French and the House of Savoy, serving as its capital from 1563, and it was during this period that it was expanded and splendid castles and hunting lodges were established around the city. When the duchy became a kingdom in 1713, first of Sicily, then Sardinia, Turin went through a further regeneration with grand buildings constructed by great architects such as Guarino Guarini (1604–83). The early 20th century gave

### DESIGNING TURIN

While Milan was long considered Italy's design capital, Turin has been an outstanding centre of industrial design for more than half a century, and has recently and quite literally stolen the title. Around half the cars on the road worldwide have had design input from the companies of Turin and Piemonte. Why? Firstly, the design firms are small and flexible, and the lack of hierarchy means they work fast. Secondly, Giugiaro, Pininfarina and Bertone (the great car designers) have been 'coach makers' as well – meaning they actually made car bodywork and understood manufacturing.

the city some exquisite Art Nouveau architecture, while the 1930s were when many of the arcades were constructed.

Named World Design Capital in 2008, Turin is also one of Italy's hippest and most cultured cities, with over 40 great museums, scores of art and design galleries, a creative young university crowd, a buzzy café and *aperitivo* scene, and dozens of chic fashion and design stores.

Turin's tourism departments have really got their act together since the city hosted the 2006 Winter Olympics, and you can expect tourist offices to inundate you with information, a range of discount passes and a long list of themed tours including gastronomic and *aperitivi* tours, art, literary and film-oriented tours and walks to enjoy the city's statues and monuments.

The ChocoPass, for instance, enables you to visit a number of chocolate stores to sample local specialities, while a Gourmet booklet includes a number

*Piemonte and Valle d'Aosta*

Piemonte and Valle d'Aosta

Caffè Mulafsano (see p157) is one of the most famous cafés in Turin

of local restaurants offering fixed-price set menus focused on regional specialities. The Torino+Piemonte Card gives you free transport and free entry to 160 museums, exhibitions, castles, fortresses and palaces in Turin and the Piemonte region and discounts on tours. The tourist offices also offer tours taking in museums and sights. One, for instance, enables you to discover the architecture of Guarino Guarini, Filippo Juvarra and Alessandro Antonelli.

## Chiesa di San Lorenzo
### (San Lorenzo Church)

This lovely church was designed by revered architect Guarino Guarini, also responsible for the Duomo di San Giovanni (see below). It is a very appealing building – mainly due to its symmetrical lines, dramatic interior and atmospheric mood created by the filtered light.

*Piazza Castello. Tel: (011) 436 15 27.*
*Open: 9am–noon & 4–7pm.*
*Free admission.*

## Duomo di San Giovanni
### (Cathedral of Saint John)

Turin's austere 15th-century Renaissance cathedral, dedicated to Saint John the Baptist, is home to the black marble Cappella della Sacra Sindone (Chapel of the Holy Shroud), designed by celebrated architect Guarino Guarini to house that famous piece of linen, which was exhibited here until a fire struck the church in 1997. The shroud underwent extensive restoration in 2002 to remove patches that had been sewn on centuries earlier, and is now exhibited in the Royal Chapel. Thought by many to be the burial shroud of Jesus of Nazareth, it's a topic that has been hotly debated over the years, with different independent teams of scientists placing its creation in the Middle Ages. The cathedral has been undergoing restoration ever since the fire; the dome was being restored at the time of research.

*Piazza San Giovanni.*
*Tel: (011) 436 15 40. Open: 9am–noon*
*& 3–7pm. Free admission.*

## Galleria Civica d'Arte Moderna e Contemporanea
## (Civic Gallery of Modern and Contemporary Art) (GAM)

The museum's collection comprises over 50,000 works, with paintings from the late 18th and 19th centuries and art works from the 20th century to the present. While there is a definite focus on art from Turin, Piemonte and Italy, there are also works from the international arena. Particularly impressive is the Italian Experimental Museum work, dating from the 1960s, and a collection of *Arte Povera* (Poor Art), along with Neo-Dada and Pop Art.
*Via Magenta 31. Tel: (011) 442 96 10.*
*www.gamtorino.it.*
*Open: Tue–Sun 10am–6pm.*
*Admission charge.*

## Galleria Sabauda (Savoy Gallery)

One of Italy's foremost art museums, it is home to the colossal collections from the House of Savoy. While there are some splendid Italian works on display and particularly fine pieces by Filippino Lippi, Andrea Mantegna and Paolo Veronese, for many the highlights come from an impressive selection of works by the Flemish masters, including Van Eyck and Memling.
*Via Accademia delle Scienza 6.*
*Tel: (011) 564 17 48.*

*www.museitorino.it. Open: Tue, Fri–Sun*
*8.30am–2pm, Wed & Thur 2–7pm.*
*Closed: Mon. Admission charge (joint*
*ticket with Museo Egizio).*

## Mole Antonelliana & Museo Nazionale del Cinema
## (National Cinema Museum)

With its elegant spire and unique square dome visible from most parts of the city, this splendid building designed by architect Alessandro Antonelli easily entices visitors to its elevator to enjoy

Mole Antonelliana is a major landmark in Turin

Piemonte and Valle d'Aosta

what must be some of the most spectacular views in Italy. Equally fascinating for film buffs is the museum's vast film collection, especially its early cinema collection, one of the world's most important. The interactive exhibition takes you for a stroll through the many different periods of cinema.
*Via Montebello 20. Tel: (011) 813 85 60. www.museonazionaledelcinema.org. Open: Tue–Fri & Sun 9am–8pm & Sat 9am–11pm. Closed: Mon. Admission charge.*

### Museo Egizio (Egyptian Museum)
Founded in 1824 by King Carlo Felice, this brilliant museum is considered to be the world's largest and most important Egyptian Museum after the museum in Cairo. Displaying 5,268 objects gathered by Bernardino Drovetti, as well as objects found on archaeological digs by Italian teams in 1900 and 1935, this is a truly outstanding collection. Important works include painted linen from 3700 BC, mummified

Inside Palazzo Reale

human remains from 2400 BC that were discovered intact with furniture, clothing, cosmetics and even food, and hundreds of masks, figurines, and statues of pharaohs, such as a particularly fine diorite statue of a seated King Ramses II, dating to 1279 BC.
*Via Accademia delle Scienza 6. Tel: (011) 561 77 76. www.museitorino.it. Open: Tue–Sun 8.30am–7.30pm. Closed: Mon. Admission charge (joint ticket with Galleria Sabauda).*

### Museo Nazionale dell'Automobile (National Automobile Museum)
A must for car enthusiasts and design fans, this fantastic museum features one of the finest car collections in the world, beginning from antique vehicles from 1896, through collections of Bugattis, Ferraris and Fiats from the history of car manufacturing. What makes the museum really stand out are its innovative temporary exhibitions, such as the Made in Italy dual exhibition that compared the connections between Italian furniture and vehicle design. Note that at the time of research, the Museum's permanent home at Corso Unità d'Italia 40 was closed for restoration and reorganisation, but a series of temporary exhibitions from the collection is planned until the museum resumes normal operations sometime during 2009.
*Torino Esposizioni, Corso Massimo D'Azeglio 15 (temporary address). Tel: (011) 659 98 72. www.museoauto.it. Open: Tue–Sun 10am–6.30pm. Closed:*

Palazzo Madama is home to a collection of fascinating objets d'art

*Mon. Admission charge. Bus to permanent museum, when reopened: 34 from Via Nizza.*

## Palazzo Madama & Museo Civico di Arte Antica
### (Turin's Civic Museum of Ancient Art)

Founded in 1860 in the Baroque Palazzo Madama, the former home of Maria Christina, queen of Savoy, this museum exhibits beautiful hand-crafted pieces of all periods, such as iron, bronze and brass works, ivory, ceramics, paintings, sculpture, furniture, costumes, jewellery, tapestries, wooden carvings, illuminated manuscripts and much more. Allow plenty of time.

*Piazza Castello. Tel: (011) 443 35 01. www.palazzomadamatorino.it. Open: Tue–Fri & Sun 10am–6pm, Sat 10am–8pm. Closed: Mon. Admission charge.*

## Palazzo Reale (Royal Palace)

The sumptuous 17th-century palace behind the enormous gates on Piazzetta Reale was once the headquarters of the capital of the Duchy of Savoy, where some of the greatest historical decisions were made. Take a stroll in the courtyard and around the gardens or join a guided tour of the lavish interior. *Piazzetta Reale. Tel: (011) 436 14 55. Open: Tue–Sun 9am–6pm. Closed: Mon. Admission charge.*

# Walk: Turin stroll

*This leisurely stroll along Turin's grand boulevards and charming backstreets gives you a good feel for this glorious city while taking in its key sights. The walk is structured in such a way that if you are taking the full day you should arrive at Mole Antonelliana in the late afternoon to enjoy the exquisite light.*

*Allow 2 hours for the walk at a casual pace; however, you can stretch it to a full day if you stop en route.*

*Begin your exploration at leafy Piazza Carlo Felice, in front of Stazione Porta Nuova.*

## 1 Via Roma: Piazza Carlo Felice

The Piazza's splendid buildings and imposing arcades offer a taste of things to come.

*Stroll through the arcades of Via Roma to Piazza San Carlo.*

## 2 Via Roma: Piazza San Carlo

Turin's most prestigious shopping street, Via Roma is lined with chic shops, from Italian fashion boutiques Promod and Calzedonia to swish designer stores Dolce&Gabbana, Emilio Pucci and Georgio Armani.

*Continue along Via Roma to Piazza Castello. Turn left on Via Barbaroux.*

## 3 Via Barbaroux

This pedestrian-only street leads into a charming quarter of old-fashioned shops, gourmet food stores, hippy boutiques, herbalists, cafés, bars and pubs. It's particularly lively in the evenings. Explore the area before making your way to pedestrian Via Garibaldi, lined with mainstream shops.

*From Via Boreto turn right on Via Garibaldi then left on Via Milano to Piazza Palazzo di Città.*

## 4 Piazza Palazzo di Città (City Hall)

This splendid piazza is home to the distinguished City Hall and several atmospheric cafés.

*Stroll along Via Palazzo di Città to the intersection of Piazzetta Reale and Piazza Castello.*

A statue at the Palazzo di Città

## 5 Piazzetta Reale (Royal Palace) and Piazza Castello

These two grand squares, one traffic-free (Piazzetta Reale) and one chaotic with traffic (Piazza Castello), are home to the tourist office and key sights such as Palazzo Madama, Chiesa di San Lorenzo, Palazzo Reale and nearby San Giovanni Duomo (*see pp28–9 & 31*).
*Cross Piazza Castello and head down Via Accademia delle Scienza, home to Galleria Sabauda, to Piazza Carlo Alberto.*

## 6 Piazza Carlo Alberto

The attractive pedestrian streets around Piazza Carlo Alberto are lively at lunch time and in the evening when the cafés, restaurants and bars around here are crammed with people.

*Stroll through Galleria Subalpina to Via Po. Follow Via Po to Via Sant'Ottavio.*

## 7 Mole Antonelliana and Museo del Cinema

*See pp29–30.*
*Return to Via Po and walk a block to Piazza Vittorio Veneto.*

## 8 Piazza Vittorio Veneto

This is one of Turin's loveliest squares, home to more restaurants, cafés and bars, and an art-house cinema. It hums at *aperitivo* time when the locals sit back and enjoy the views across the river to Chiesa della Gran Madre di Dio (Church of the Mother of God), Monte dei Cappuccini (Mount of the Capuchins) and the lush foothills.

*Walk: Turin stroll*

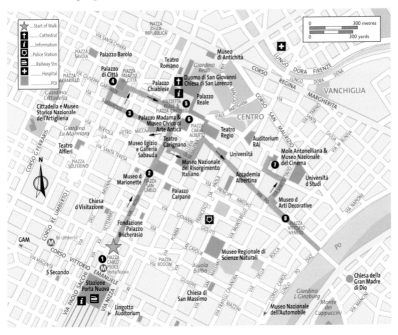

Piemonte and Valle d'Aosta

Porta Pretoria is one of the original Roman structures in Aosta

## Aosta

The Romans were the first to appreciate this strategic location – Aosta is at the crossroads of two of the most historically important trade routes between Italy and France – and this small, attractive Alpine city in the heart of the Valle d'Aosta is one of the best examples of an ancient Roman urban centre, with its well-preserved Roman city walls and streets, and its Arco di Augusto (Arch of Augustus) dating to 25 BC.

The cobblestone streets of the historic centre are a lovely place for a stroll, with a few medieval gems. The 10th-century **Duomo** has an elaborate Gothic interior while the 11th-century **Collegiata di Sant'Orso** (Collegiate Church of Saint Orso) features beautiful frescoes (you need to ask to see them) and a pretty

12th-century cloister with 40 stone columns intricately carved. Make sure to leave time for some shopping. Aosta's pedestrian streets are lined with *enoteche* (wine shops where you can taste the goods), and gourmet grocery stores.

Don't miss the **Teatro Romano** façade and the ruins of the ancient amphitheatre, built in the 1st century BC, which would have seated 20,000 spectators, and the enormous Roman **Porta Pretoria** with its impressive massive gates.

### Parco Nazionale del Gran Paradiso (**National Park of Gran Paradiso**)

This wonderful National Park is one of Europe's oldest and also one of its most ruggedly beautiful. The area once belonged to King Vittorio Emanuele III who gave it to Italy after World War I. There's a wealth of flora and fauna in the park, such as the rare ibex, and the place is blanketed with wildflowers in spring. The park offers an array of outdoor activities that you can undertake independently or with guides on organised excursions where all equipment is provided, including hiking, climbing, canyoning, mountaineering, horse riding, mountain biking, kayaking and rafting, and themed nature excursions from photographic wildlife safaris to nocturnal astronomical tours. The tourist office in Aosta has loads of information on the park, guided hikes and tours, but the main gateway to the park is the town of Cogne.

## WINTER WONDERLANDS

Northern Italy has several great ski areas, with either fascinating histories or just wonderful ski runs. The Valle d'Aosta region has charming Courmayeur on the opposite side of Monte Bianco (Mont Blanc) from Chamonix, France, where you can take the world's most famous ski run, the 'Vallée Blanche'. Cervinia is on the opposite side of the Matterhorn from delightful Zermatt, Switzerland, and you can cross the mountains to ski Zermatt and be back for dinner. The Italian Dolomites has a former Olympic resort in spectacular Cortina d'Ampezzo and the massive Dolomite Superski region. Another Olympic ski area is around Turin (host of the 2006 games), called The Milky Way.

*Park office: Via Bourgeois 34, Cogne. Tel: (0165) 74 040. www.cogne.org. Open: daily 9am–noon, Mon–Sat also 3–6pm.*
*Tourist office: Piazza Chanoux 2, Aosta. Tel: (0165) 236 627. www.regione.vda.it. Open: Jun–Oct daily 9am–8pm; Nov–May Mon–Sat 9.30am–6.30pm, Sun 9.30am–1pm.*

### Alba

Once known as the 'city of a hundred towers', Alba is now more noted for its sublime white truffles found in the hills around town, as well as for its wine and chocolate (it's the home of the Ferrero confectionery company). Although there are no longer one hundred, the remaining sky-scraping 14th- to 15th-century towers seem to surprise you at every turn.

Established on the site of Alba Pompeia in 89 BC, you can still see some remains of the ancient Roman city, including ruined city walls and fortified gate, and mosaics. Alba's main sights include the 13th-century **Palazzo Comunale**, **Bishop's Palace** and several impressive churches, including the 12th-century red-brick Romanesque **Duomo** or **Cathedral of San Lorenzo** (*Piazza Risorgimento. Tel: (0173) 440 000. Free admission*), which has a gorgeous carved wooden chorus crafted by Bernardino Fossati in 1512 and an enormous bell tower. During summer there are often concerts in the adjacent piazza.

The 13th-century Gothic **Chiesa di San Domenico** (Church of Saint Dominic) has a beautiful portal and faded Renaissance frescoes, while the Baroque **Chiesa di San Giovanni** (Church of Saint John the Baptist) has fine paintings by Macrino d'Alba and Barnaba da Modena.

Alba's Duomo

## WHITE GOLD

As autumn approaches sleepy Alba, locals become animated about the upcoming *tuber magnatum* season, the hunt for an ugly, pale-cream, dirt-covered growth between the size of a marble and a cricket ball – the Alba white truffle. From September to December, local truffle hunters, *trifulau*, can earn a year's wages as their dogs sniff out these gems around the roots of oak, hazel, poplar and beech trees in the local forests. As they can't be cultivated and have a distinctive smell and taste, this culinary delight goes for anywhere between €2,000 and €4,000 per kilo. A pasta dish with some freshly shaved local white truffle can cost up to €100.

## Asti

Splendidly situated in the lovely Langhe and Monferrato hill region, Asti is famous for its sparkling wine Asti Spumante, robust red wines Barolo, Barbaresco and Barbera d'Asti, and its white truffle (*tartufo bianco*). It's also beloved by Italians for its annual medieval equestrian event and pageant, held in September, the bareback horse race, the Palio d'Asti, and its regional food and wine festival, the Festival delle Sagre.

Like Piemonte's other towns, Asti also has its fair share of beautiful historic churches, including the monumental 13th-century Romanesque-Gothic cathedral, one of the largest churches in the region, the **Cattedrale di Santa Maria Assunta** (Cathedral of Our Lady of the Assumption. *Piazza Cattedrale. Tel: (0141) 592 924. Open: daily 8.30am–noon & 3.30–5.30pm. Free admission*), which boasts an equally

colossal belfry. The façade features three portals and three rose windows. Inside, there are some lovely 18th-century frescoes. Other churches worth checking out are the 13th-century **Collegiata di San Secondo** (*Piazza San Secondo. Tel: (0141) 530 066. Open: daily 10.30am–noon & 3.30–5.30pm. Free admission*) with its 6th-century crypt, and the 12th-century octagonal **Battistero di San Pietro** (Baptistery of Saint Peter). There is also a good Archaeological Museum displaying mainly Roman relics.

## Barolo

This pretty village, famed for its winemaking and big bold Barolo reds, also boasts a remarkable castle, **Castello Falletti** (*Piazza Falletti. Tel: (0173) 56 277. Open: Mon–Wed & Fri–Sun 10am–6pm. Closed: Thur & Jan. Admission charge for castle, enoteca free*), whose sumptuously decorated rooms are filled with antiques and art, and hosts a regional *enoteca*, an excellent spot for sampling local wines. Barolo is also home to a quirky museum, the **Museo dei Cavatappi** (Corkscrew Museum) *Piazza Castello 4. Tel: (0173) 560 539. www.museodeicavatappi.it. Open: daily 10am–1pm & 2–6pm. Closed: Jan & Feb. Admission charge*) and lots of gastronomic stores, selling delicious local products and, naturally, wine.

## Saluzzo

Sprawled on a hilltop, this affluent town – wealthy from the marble, slate, iron and silver found in the surrounding mountains – has enigmatic winding streets, buildings painted with trompe-l'œil scenes, grand Renaissance *palazzi* and gorgeous Gothic churches.

Saluzzo's star attraction is the Lombardi-Gothic **Duomo**, dating from 1491, which has a stunning façade decorated with faded frescoes, statues and rose windows, and a beautiful Baroque altar. The Gothic **Chiesa di San Giovanni** (Church of Saint John) (*Open: daily 10am–1pm & 3.30–6pm.*

*Free admission*) is even older, dating to 1330, although it wasn't completed until 1504, and boasts fine Renaissance paintings by Antoine Le Moiturier, Benedetto Briosco and Matteo Sanmicheli. The **Chiesa di San Bernardo** (Church of Saint Bernard) (*Open: daily 10am–1pm & 3.30–6pm. Free admission*) is home to the splendid tombs of the della Torre counts. Don't miss the restored Renaissance interior of the **Casa Cavassa** (*Via San Giovanni 5*) and the elegant late Renaissance décor of the 16th-century **Villa Belvedere**.

The Cattedrale di Santa Maria Assunta in Asti

# Northern Italian wines

Northern Italian wines are, by any standards, excellent. The famous big red, Barolo, is made here, as is the increasingly popular white, Pinot Grigio.

Just like France, *terroir* (the characteristics of the land) is important and the Italians have a wine classification system similar to the French. *Denominazione di Origine Controllata* (DOC) and *Denominazione di Origine Controllata et Garantita* (DOCG) guarantee that the wines are from the specified area, with DOCG an additional guarantee of quality.

*Indicazione Geografica Tipica* (IGT) simply means a wine typical of the region, while *Vino da Tavola* (table wine) is the lowest category. However, some of Italy's best wines have been in the 'table wine' category – famously the so-called 'super-Tuscans', because their use of grapes or winemaking techniques falls outside the regulations.

In the northwest, the region of Piemonte has over 50 DOC-DOCG zones and is home to Italy's most respected wine, Barolo. Made from Nebbiolo grapes (the main grape of the region), the wine is tannic when young, and Barolos are generally aged between 7–10 years, with great vintages drinkable at 20. Another great red, Barbaresco, is less expensive and drinks well between 5–10 years. Another red is Barbera, with both Barbera d'Alba and Barbera d'Asti worth trying. Also from Asti is the much-maligned Asti Spumante, a sparkling, sweet, low-alcohol wine made from the Moscato grape.

Early-season grapes in Trentino-Alto Adige

Barolo is considered the best wine in Italy

In other regions of the northwest, much of Lombardia's production goes to bulk wine, but the sparkling DOCG wines of Franciacorta are notable, as are the Nebbiolo-based reds of the Valtellina region. Valle d'Aosta's wine-growing region's high altitude sees some interesting wines, such as the DOC wines Donnaz and Enfer d'Arvier, both respectable reds. In Emilia-Romagna, a lighter red, Lambrusco, is popular – the exported varieties are generally sweet and cloying – while the local dry versions (usually DOC) match the local cooking beautifully.

In the northeast, the region of the Veneto is one of the most important and produces the most wine in Italy. Much is exported, including plenty of IGT wines, but the trio of Soave, Bardolino and Valpolicella is notable. Soave, a generally dry white made from Garganega and Trebbiano di Soave, is one of Italy's most popular whites, and, while many are average, some transcend. Bardolino comes from a mix of grape varieties, Corvina, Rondinella Molinara and Negrara, and is a dry, sometimes bitter, wine, drunk young. A typical Valpolicella is an easy and early-drinking red, but varieties such as the Amarone della Valpolicella (made with air-dried grapes) are more interesting. The sparkling wine you'll see in glasses clinked everywhere, Prosecco, is also from the region.

Trentino-Alto Adige is known for its Pinot Grigio (Pinot Gris), a light, delicate white, but the high altitude also sees Gewürztraminer, Müller Thurgau and white Moscato being produced – all of which can be good quality. Friuli-Venezia Giulia has been dominated by Tocai Friulano, but the EU ruled that this name is too close to Tokaji of Hungary. Friulano is an elegant, floral white when at its best.

# Liguria and Emilia-Romagna

*Lovely Liguria and elegant Emilia-Romagna are two of Italy's most culturally rich, stylish and sophisticated regions, with fine art, design, music and museums in abundance, and epicurean delights to satisfy the most discerning taste buds. They also boast some of Northern Italy's most beautiful landscapes, with beaches, bucolic countryside and spectacular coastal scenery.*

In Liguria there's the majestic coastline of the Cinque Terre with its craggy cliffs, vine-covered slopes and network of hiking trails connecting the pretty villages; the charming Riviera di Levante, home to the Cinque Terre and colourful fishing villages and family holiday destinations that stretch from Camogli in the north to Portovenere in the south; and the Riviera di Ponente, typically Mediterranean in its beauty with a sparkling turquoise sea,

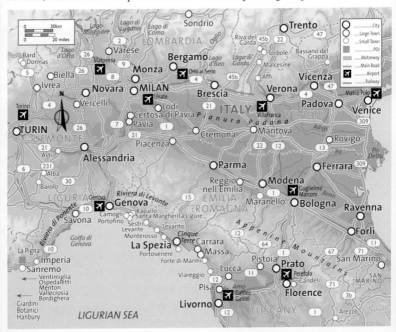

luxuriant villa gardens, and grand palm-lined esplanades that are more French Riviera in look and feel than Italian. In Emilia-Romagna, on the other hand, the landscapes vary from the rugged, wild country of the Apennine Mountains, to the idyllic undulating hills of the Pianura Padana farms with their dirt driveways lined with rows of poplars.

Sharing its border with France to the west, the regions of Piemonte to the north and Emilia-Romagna in the east, and stretching to the shimmering Mediterranean Sea in the south, Liguria is home to some of Italy's most glamorous destinations, from fashionable Portofino, long popular with Hollywood A-list stars, to retro Sanremo, the *grande dame* of Italy's beach resorts.

By contrast, Liguria's capital, Genova, once an important stop for European aristocrats on their Grand Tours, is a gritty port city with a seedy quality to the skinny backstreets of its old town. Nevertheless, it also boasts grand squares dominated by striking black-and-white striped churches, enormous elegant arcades shading shiny marble floors, and most impressive museums set in imposing mansions. There's also excellent shopping, superb restaurants and a lively *aperitivo* scene.

Bounded by the regions of Liguria and Piemonte in the west, Lombardia in the north, the calm Adriatic Sea in the east, and Tuscany (Toscana) and Marche in the south, Emilia-Romagna in turn is home to some of Italy's most affluent and refined cities. Ravenna, Ferrara and Modena all boast marble pedestrian streets, sumptuous cathedrals and elegant squares, while Parma and Bologna, with their gourmet food shops, fine wine stores and vibrant bars, must be the region's gastronomic capitals. All of the cities have an intellectual and cultural life that is the envy of others, while the mood during the summer music concert season has many visitors checking the property prices in the estate agents' windows.

Like all Italian regions, Liguria and Emilia-Romagna have long, rich histories. Liguria's history centres on Genova, a city that prides itself on its success at sea, through voyages of exploration, maritime trade, colonial endeavours, piracy, politics and, of course, religion. A significant trading post as far back as the 3rd century, it was from Genova's port that the Crusaders departed for the East, and Genoese Christopher Columbus set sail. The two provinces of Emilia and Romagna formed the Papal States following the Fall of the Roman Empire, Ravenna was capital of the Western Roman Empire for a while when it was lavishly decorated, while the cities of both provinces were important centres during the artistic flourishing of the Renaissance period under the powerful and eccentric Este dynasty.

## LIGURIA
### Genova

Genova is one of Northern Italy's most fascinating and most surprising cities. Its perfectly preserved medieval historic centre is equally as graceful and elegant as it is seamy and rough around the edges. The city has a vibrant atmosphere more akin to the Middle Eastern flavour of Naples in the South than the elegance and refinement of quintessential Northern Italian cities such as Turin or Milan.

Long a port city, lively Genova was the departure point for some of Italy's most successful historic voyages and home to some of the country's most

Teatro Carlo Felice (*see p47*)

### GENOVA'S PORT

It's fitting that the birthplace of the famous explorer Christopher Columbus (1451) is a classic port town. Originally a small fishing port, it was already a trading centre with a significant merchant fleet by 934 when it was attacked and sacked by Arab pirates. This seafaring heritage saw Genova considered as a 'Maritime Republic', an independent city-state, along with other cities such as Venice. Trade and shipbuilding were the biggest industries and the city won naval battles with both Pisa (1284) and Venice (1298). While sea trade brought prosperity (as witnessed by the architectural heritage), it also brought the Black Death in 1349. Today the port serves as the chief export point of much of Northern Italy's agricultural and industrial products.

admired explorers and adventures, including Christopher Columbus. Venetian Marco Polo also spent some time here – under lock and key in the fortress of the Palazzo di San Giorgio (Palace of Saint George) where he wrote (with the help of scribe Rustichello) *The Travels of Marco Polo*.

While Genova's once filthy, crime-ridden docks have been cleaned up in recent years as part of a revitalisation programme of the *Porto Antico* (old port), and shiny new museums and five-star hotels now reside at the port, the dingy waterfront bars off Piazza Caricamento are still dominated by drunken sailors and dodgy dealings. In the narrow, dimly lit backstreets behind the square, the languages of North and East Africa are more widely spoken than Italian. The area is as intriguing as it is intimidating.

Il Grande Bigo, constructed for the 500th anniversary of Columbus's discovery of America

Although the Old Town's atmospheric pedestrian-only lanes have undergone a welcoming gentrification, you'll still find delightfully old-fashioned cafés with tempting window displays of chocolates, chandeliers hanging from the ceilings and mirrors on the walls, alongside antique pharmacies and sweet shops with antique glass jars on their shelves and pretty photogenic shop-fronts. Most of the previously ramshackle stores have been renovated and converted to chic boutiques, hip bars and sleek restaurants.

Via San Lorenzo and its narrow side streets are lined with stylish shops, from trendy fashion franchises to exclusive designer stores, the lanes around Piazza Soziglia are the place to find well-regarded restaurants, while Piazza delle Erbe is the location of a handful of buzzy bars and one of the North's best *aperitivo* scenes. Once known as Genova's 'Street of Gold', Via Garibaldi still retains an unrivalled elegance with its lavish Renaissance and Rococo palaces, now home to some of the city's best museums, which give an insight into Genova's former wealth.

Unusual black-and-white decoration on the Cattedrale di San Lorenzo

## Cattedrale di San Lorenzo
(**Saint Lawrence Cathedral**)

This grand black-and-white striped cathedral with its splendid façade of fluted columns and intricate decoration is the first stop for most visitors to Genova, who tend to find themselves lingering for some time on the marble steps of the splendid church. The striking stripes, which you'll also notice on other churches and buildings in Genova, are created from alternating layers of fine Carrara marble and slate, and were a symbol of the city's wealth. Inside there are attractive Byzantine frescoes, and a Renaissance chapel, which, legend has it, once housed the ashes of Saint John the Baptist.

*Piazza Matteotti, Via San Lorenzo.*
*Open: 7am–7pm daily. Free admission.*

## Museo d'Arte Orientale
(**Museum of Oriental Art**)

Edoardo Chiossone, patron of this impressive museum, was an avid art collector who, while residing in Japan for 23 years during the Meiji period, developed an extensive and eclectic collection of some 20,000 Japanese artefacts, precious objects and art, including paintings, prints, sculptures, statues, ceramics, coins, costumes and musical instruments. The most impressive exhibitions are a room full of beautiful Buddhist statues, and Galerie 2, which features decorative

objects including theatrical masks, miniature wooden sculptures and intricately detailed lacquerware.
*Villetta Di Negro, Piazzale Mazzini 4. Tel: (010) 542 285.*
*www.museochiossonegenova.it. Open: Tue–Fri 9am–1pm, Sat–Sun 10am–7pm. Closed: Mon. Admission charge.*

## Museo delle Culture del Mondo (Museum of World Cultures)

Situated in the splendid 19th-century Castello d'Albertis, an imposing fortification built by Captain Enrico Alberto d'Albertis (1846–1932) whose fascinating collection now fills the castle's rooms, this compelling museum of ethnography is one of the best of its kind. A traveller, adventurer, amateur archaeologist, naturalist and hunter, Genoese sailor Captain d'Albertis amassed an enormous collection of artefacts, precious objects, souvenirs, nautical paraphernalia and hunting trophies from Africa, the Americas, Asia and Oceania. Highlights include pre-Columbian pottery and textiles, archaeological artefacts from the Mayans and Aztecs, and a fascinating 'cabinet of curiosities'. One of the most enjoyable exhibitions is one dedicated to the instruments, sounds and music of an array of world cultures.
*Corso Dogali 18. Tel: (010) 272 38 20. www.castellodalbertisgenova.it. Open: Oct–Mar Tue–Fri 10am–5pm, Sat–Sun 10am–6pm; Apr–Sept Sat–Sun 10am–7pm. Closed: Mon. Admission charge.*

### PERFECTING PESTO

Genova's most famous and tastiest export is *pesto alla genovese* – in English it's just generally know as pesto. There are other types of pesto, but the real deal is made with Genovese basil, which is crushed in a mortar with some salt and garlic until it forms a cream. Pine nuts, usually lightly toasted, are added, then grated Parmigiano and Pecorino cheeses, and lastly Ligurian extra-virgin olive oil.

## Musei di Strada Nuova (Museums of the 'Golden Street')

These three sumptuous palaces on Via Garibaldi, the Palazzo Rosso (Red Palace), Palazzo Bianco (White Palace) and Palazzo Tursi (Palace of the Duke of Tursi), house magnificent collections of Italian art from the 15th to the 19th centuries in lavish rooms. The original Rococo décor and antique furniture that once belonged to the Brignole-Sale family is almost as impressive as the art on the walls. Don't miss the 'Seasons' rooms, resplendent with vivid Genoese Baroque frescoes, in Palazzo Rosso, the collections of Flemish art including works by Rubens and Van Dyck, Italian paintings by the great artists Veronese and Caravaggio, and a rich collection of 17th-century tapestries at Palazzo Tursi.
*Palazzo Rosso, Via Garibaldi 18; Palazzo Bianco, Via Garibaldi 11; Palazzo Tursi, Via Garibaldi 9. Tel: (010) 247 63 51. www.stradanuova.it. Open: Tue–Fri 9am–7pm, Sat & Sun 10am–7pm. Closed: Mon. Admission charge (one ticket for all three sites).*

Liguria and Emilia-Romagna

# Walk: Genova's highlights

*This hike through Genova's labyrinthine old town takes in elegant squares, narrow lanes, the rejuvenated waterfront and the city's 'Golden Street'. Genova's tangle of medieval streets in the* centro storico *can be confusing for first-time visitors but getting lost is part of the fun. Prepare for a rigorous walk, as Genova's streets are hilly.*

*Allow 2 hours for the walk and up to a full day if you take time out to visit the museums. Start at Piazza de Ferrari.*

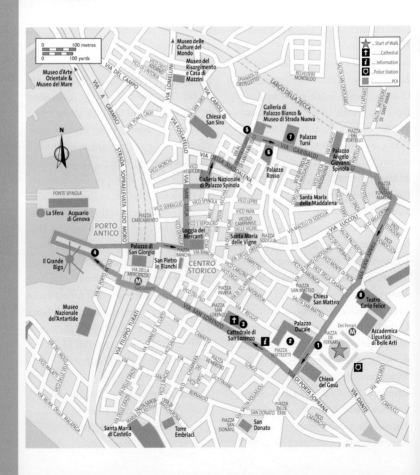

## 1 Piazza de Ferrari

This square is a popular meeting place with locals. The best views of the Palazzo Ducale are from the fountain.
*Follow Via Cardinale Boetto to Piazza Matteotti and Palazzo Ducale.*

## 2 Palazzo Ducale

Admire Palazzo Ducale from another perspective before heading inside to see what exhibitions are on.
*Piazza Matteotti. Tel: (010) 557 40 64. Open: Tue–Sun 10am–7pm. Closed: Mon. Admission charge. Follow Via San Lorenzo to Piazza San Lorenzo.*

## 3 Cattedrale di San Lorenzo (Saint Lawrence Cathedral)

*See p44.*
*Continue along Via San Lorenzo, the old town's main pedestrian shopping street.*

## 4 Marina Porto Antico (Old Port Marina)

The rejuvenated waterfront is more appealing now than a decade ago when many were too scared to venture here. There's a small ethnic market and several attractions, including **Museo del Mare** (Museum of the Sea) (*Tel: (010) 234 56 55. www.galatamuseodelmare.it. Open: Tue–Sun 10am–6pm. Closed: Mon. Admission charge*) and **Acquario di Genova** (Aquarium) (*Tel: (010) 234 56 66. www.acquariodigenova.it. Open: daily 8.30am–10pm. Admission charge*).
*Take Viale Ponte Reale, turn left into Via San Luca, right then left again into Viale Pellicorria, right onto Via della Maddalena, and left onto Via 4 Canti San Francesco for Via Garibaldi. This labyrinth of alleys is the 'Caruggi', the gritty medieval heart of the historic centre (beware of pickpockets).*

## 5 Via Garibaldi and Palazzo Bianco (White Palace)

Via Garibaldi was known as the 'Golden Street' (Via Aurea) in the 1550s after land was subdivided and sold to affluent Genoese families who built sumptuous palaces here. Several are superb museums, including the classical Palazzo Bianco (*see p45*).
*Stay on Via Garibaldi.*

## 6 Palazzo Rosso (Red Palace)

Diagonally opposite is Palazzo Rosso (*see p45*), built by the Brignole Sale dynasty in the 1670s.
*Stay on Via Garibaldi.*

## 7 Palazzo Tursi (Palace of the Duke of Tursi)

Palazzo Tursi is the largest of Via Garibaldi's grand palaces. Built between 1565 and 1579 by successful banker Niccolò Grimaldi, it is now Genova's city hall. (*See also p45.*)
*Continue to the end of Via Garibaldi, then cross Piazza delle Fontane Marose to Via XXV Aprile and Piazza de Ferrari.*

## 8 Teatro Carlo Felice

This is Genova's main opera house and also hosts ballets and concerts.
*Piazza de Ferrari. Tel: (010) 589 329 (Ticket office). www.carlofelice.it*

## Riviera di Ponente

An attractive, sun-drenched coastline stretching west of Genova to the French border, the Riviera di Ponente boasts palm-lined promenades, grand old hotels and a laid-back atmosphere, more reminiscent of the French Riviera than the typical bustling Italian lido-dominated resorts.

While not as glamorous as the French Riviera, the towns of the Riviera di Ponente have a similar easy-going charm. Villages tumble down craggy mountains, their houses perched atop sheer cliffs and set in luxuriant gardens overlooking the turquoise sea. Down by the beaches, gelato-coloured houses feature balconies and window shutters to block out the scorching midday heat.

### Giardini Botanici Hanbury (Hanbury Botanic Gardens)

These botanical gardens, 5km (3 miles) west of Ventimiglia, are one of the most visited attractions on the Riviera di Ponente. Established in 1867 by Sir Thomas Hanbury, a successful English merchant, the luxuriant terraced gardens are spectacularly set, hugging the hillside and overlooking the sparkling sea. Parking is a challenge. *La Mortola, Ventimiglia. Tel: (0184) 229 507. www.amicihanbury.com. Open: Mar–Jun daily 10am–5pm; Jul–Sept daily 10am–6pm; Oct–Feb Tue–Sun 9.30am–4pm. Admission charge.*

### Sanremo

Splendidly set on the Mediterranean Sea west of Genova, and considered to be the *grande dame* of Italian beach resorts, Sanremo has a certain faded grandeur not found in other seaside towns, largely due to the elegant old hotels that dominate its seaside boulevard.

Sanremo's rule at various times by Genoese bishops, the powerful De Mari and Doria dynasties, the French Savoys and the Kingdom of Sardinia, is evident in a few attractions, including the small but well-preserved *centro storico*, Basilica di San Siro (Saint Siro's Basilica) and Forte di Santa Tecla (Fortress of Saint Tecla).

Sanremo beach

What is most striking to visitors is the imposing architecture from the town's heyday, which began in the 19th century when travellers first started setting off on their Grand Tours of Europe – and equally grand hotels were established on the seafront to accommodate them – and continued until World War II. While the hotels aren't as lavish as they once were, their opulent interiors provide an insight into the splendour of 19th- and 20th-century travel and are worth a peek if you aren't checking into one. The most famous of all is the majestic Royal Hotel Sanremo, set in verdant gardens lush with bougainvillea and towering palm trees.

The most frequent of the many visitors to Sanremo was the Russian Empress Maria Alexandrovna. The Romanovs spent considerable time here escaping the icy Russian winter, and as a result the town has attracted Russians ever since, as evident by the exotic onion-domed **Chiesa Russa Ortodossa** (Russian Orthodox Church) opposite the waterfront near the Royal Hotel, built in 1912 for Sanremo's Russian community (*Via Nuvoloni 2. Tel: (0184) 531 807. Open: daily 9.30am–12.30pm & 3–6pm. Free admission*).

Sanremo is also famous for its music festivals (*see p18*) and hosts a solid programme of jazz, classical music, opera and theatre throughout the year, with most concerts held throughout summer. The tourist office can provide details (*Via Nuvolini 1. Tel: (0184) 59059. www.rivieradeifiori.com. Open: Mon–Sat*

The onion domes of Sanremo's Russian Orthodox Church

*8am–6.30pm (until 7pm in summer), Sun 9am–1pm*).

A popular day trip from Sanremo is to the old town of **La Pigna** (the pine cone), which has undergone extensive restoration in recent years. You can pick up the brochure from the tourist office. La Pigna is around 60km (37 miles) from Sanremo, but the road is very hilly, narrow and winding, so it can take anything up to a couple of hours to get there.

## Riviera di Levante

Riviera di Levante takes in the pretty pastel-painted seaside resorts stretching along the coast southeast of Genova, starting at Camogli and including Rapallo, Portofino, Santa Margherita Ligure, the Cinque Terre villages and Portovenere. As popular with Italians as foreigners, the towns get uncomfortably crowded in summer when it's next to impossible to find accommodation and parking, so the Riviera is best visited in spring.

## Camogli

This charming fishing village of tall, colourful houses lining the waterfront boasts an attractive beach and atmospheric little harbour where fishing boats bob in the water. Camogli has more authenticity than any other destination on this part of the coast –

Portofino's harbour

### J LO AND THE JET SET

Portofino's pretty harbour caters less for fishermen and more for huge yachts these days, its main income derived from tourism. While many come to admire the harbour, just as many appear to come for the celebrity spotting, sipping overpriced drinks while waiting for Jennifer Lopez (J Lo) to come ashore for a spot of shopping. During the warmer months, the yachts moored around the harbour become a temporary home to many famous people, from designer Tom Ford, model Naomi Campbell, singers Kylie Minogue and Bono and actresses such as Eva Longoria. While many choose to stay on board their floating palaces for the duration of their stay, you can star-spot at Restaurant Il Delfino and Bar Morena Di Ugo.

you're more likely to hear Italian spoken on the streets than English, which can't be said for other resorts. That, combined with the fact that it's far more popular with Italians than foreigners, is its appeal. The local cuisine is renowned, especially its fish and *focaccia* (thick Italian bread).

## Portofino

Separated from Camogli by the verdant 600m (1,968ft) high Monte Portofino (Portofino Mountain), this former fishing village is now a glamorous tourist resort popular with the rich and famous (*see box above*). Situated on the southeastern extremity of a densely forested mountain and set around one of Italy's prettiest harbours, Portofino was founded by the Romans, who named it Portus Delphini (Port of the Dolphin) after the dolphins that swam

The small beach at Paraggi, near Santa Margherita Ligure, can get crowded

in the bay. Part of the Republic of Genova from the 13th century, Portofino's harbour provided a safe haven for the Republic's merchant marine. Now the bay hosts the expensive yachts and sleek cruisers of celebrities and moguls.

Just like Sanremo, Portofino began to receive British and European travellers on their Grand Tour in the 19th century; by the 1950s tourism had supplanted fishing as the village's primary industry. That said, there's little to do in Portofino. In the evenings, tourists stroll the two seaside promenades, Calata Marconi and Molo Umberto I, lined with seafood restaurants, cafés and ice-cream parlours. As the nearest beach around the bay at Paraggi is tiny, by day visitors shop in Portofino's exclusive boutiques, kick back in the waterfront cafés, or

hike up the San Girgio path to medieval **Castello Brown**, named after British Consul Yeats Brown, to take in the enchanting panoramas and enjoy the fragrant rose gardens.

*Castello Brown open only for special events and functions. Gardens open, contact tourist office for details: Via Roma 35. Tel: (0185) 269 024.*

### Portovenere

Gorgeously sited at the end of a verdant peninsula on the Gulf of La Spezia, just south of the Cinque Terre, Portovenere is a delight to visit. Known to the English as the place where Lord Byron (1788–1824) stayed for a while to write and famously swam across the water to see his friend Shelley, Portovenere is more renowned among Italians for its fine seafood restaurants – a meal here is a must for lunch.

Pastel-coloured buildings by the water at Portovenere

Lolly-coloured houses, mostly now home to restaurants and cafés, line the pedestrian-only waterfront in the *centro storico* within splashing distance from the water's edge. As there's no beach at the old centre (it's a ten-minute walk along the water; expect to park up the hill and walk down as parking is largely restricted to residents only), the young Italian locals and holiday-makers like to sunbathe, flirt, and listen to music on a concrete platform nearby, making for some fascinating people-watching.

### Rapallo

Rapallo is the Sanremo of the Riviera di Potente, an old-fashioned resort with grand hotels, leafy streets, a palm-lined waterfront and a lively lido culture dominating the beach action. The town attracts big Italian families and retirees who spend their days glued to the shady park benches on the seafront Via Veneto.

Protruding out from the Via Veneto into the bay is the splendid 16th-century stone **Castello**, open for exhibitions (*check details with the tourist office on Lungomare Via Veneto, Tel: (0185) 230 03 46*). Opposite the waterfront are rows of alfresco restaurants and more ice-cream parlours than any other town on the coast. Ritualistically during summer evenings, locals and holiday-makers alike stroll the promenade with an ice cream, cross the little bridge, and wander along the narrow canal where the boats are docked.

### Santa Margherita Ligure

Santa Margherita Ligure is a refined old resort town with elegant pastel-painted Liberty buildings, swaying palm trees and alfresco cafés. Its busy marina and bay anchored with yachts attest to its popularity with well-heeled Italians, the kind of people who would head to Portofino if it weren't so full of celebrities. Yet the town is also attracting a hipper, younger set. Like Rapallo and Camogli, Santa Margherita Ligure has more of an authenticity about it and an easy-going charm – there's no need to dress up for dinner here – and yet it's still handy enough for day trips to nearby Portofino and the Cinque Terre villages.

While it's the kind of place that inspires swimming, sunbathing and book-reading and little else, there are a couple of engaging sights. Worth the hike up the hill above town is the **Chiesa di San Giacomo di Corte** (*Church of Saint James of Corte, beside Villa Durazzo. Open: daily 8.30am–noon & 3.30–7pm*), which has an ornate Baroque façade and sweeping panoramic bay vistas.

Nearby, **Villa Durazzo** boasts a vibrant paint job (crimson walls and green shutters), a richly decorated interior and luxuriant gardens with statues, fountains and mosaic-tiled paths. The villa is currently closed for renovation; to see the interior, check the opening hours with the tourist office.
*Via XXV Aprile 2/b.*
*Tel: (0185) 287 485.*

Rapallo's castle on the waterfront

Monterosso can get crowded, especially in summer

## Cinque Terre

Although first-time visitors still find the five pretty pastel-coloured villages of the Cinque Terre (Five Lands) captivating, for many, Riomaggiore, Manarola, Corniglia, Vernazza and Monterosso have sadly lost some of the ramshackle charm and laid-back appeal that first attracted intrepid backpackers and hikers in the 1970s.

While there is no denying that the villages are delightful with their colourful narrow buildings picturesquely set around sparkling bays with bobbing fishing boats, and cafés lining their waterfront, all set against a backdrop of colossal terraced slopes, these days the tiny, tumbledown, cliff-hugging villages are tremendously popular with tourists, and in summer hordes of them spill out of every train, making the villages uncomfortably

crowded. If you can, visit the villages in spring or autumn when they still have a certain allure.

The greatest appeal of the Cinque Terre is the walking trails that connect the five villages. Boasting fragrant olive-scented air, jaw-dropping views of the cobalt sea and secluded coves, majestic vineyard-covered mountains and magnificent vistas of the fairytale villages themselves (especially enchanting on first approach), completing the walk could be one of the most enjoyable and rewarding things you do in Italy. For centuries the narrow paths, carved into the steep mountainside, provided the only land access to the villages. Locals would ride their donkeys along the tracks, carting supplies or produce for sale, or carrying their provisions on their backs. These days, the trails are used mostly by recreational walkers. You will have to buy the *Cinque Terre Card*, required to walk the trail, or the *Cinque Terre Train Card*, which includes train travel between villages.

For those who enjoy driving, exploring the coast by car can be as memorable as hiking it. All of the villages are connected by road and the meandering mountain drive from one end of the Cinque Terre to the other is one of Europe's great drives. Avoid it on weekends and during holidays when Italians visit the villages and parking is next to impossible; you'll have a long sweaty walk down into the villages, and a strenuous hike back up.

As all of the villages are pedestrian-only, there is paid parking at the edge of each town, from where it's never far to walk into the centre or to the beach. If you have heavy luggage, organise with the hotel to have someone help you. If combining the drive and walk, park your car at either Riomaggiore or Monterosso al Mare (store your luggage with the hotel you plan to stay at upon your return), do the walk in one direction, then catch the train back to your car and village.

The local Genova–La Spezia train stops at each of the Cinque Terre villages every half hour or so and is a convenient option if you're more concerned with getting between towns fast than you are taking in views, as the train spends most of the time in tunnels. Buy a 24-hour Cinque Terre Tourist ticket, which allows unlimited travel between the villages (available at all stations). During the summer, ferries also run frequently to the Cinque Terre from Genova, calling in at Camogli on the way to Monterosso al Mare and Vernazza, while the Golfo dei Poeti boat departs from Portovenere for all villages.

Liguria and Emilia-Romagna

The dramatic coastline of the Cinque Terre

# Walk: Cinque Terre

*The signposted Trail number 2 (also known as Sentiero Azzuro or the Blue Trail) covers around 13km (8 miles) and is the best route to take. As the tracks can get crowded in summer and walking is limited to mornings and afternoons because of the heat, it is perhaps better to attempt the walk in spring and autumn. Wear light trekking gear: walking boots with good grip, long trousers (there are thorny bushes), a hat, and take plenty of water.*

*It is possible to do the walk in about 5–6 hours without breaks but you could easily stretch the walk to up to four days.*

*Begin the walk at Riomaggiore which you can reach by train from La Spezia.*

*Alternatively, drive there and park your car.*

## 1 Riomaggiore

Riomaggiore may not be the most beautiful village, but it has loads of

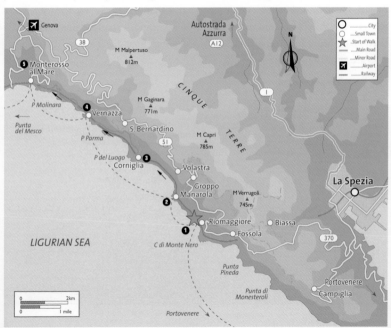

Walking trails connect the villages

morning or late afternoon on a clear day. Don't miss the 14th-century Chiesa di San Pietro (Saint Peter's Church).
*The next part of the route is fairly demanding, taking around 2 hours from Corniglia to Vernazza. The trail follows the coastline, taking you through vineyards and olive groves by stone walls, and across tiny bridges over trickling brooks – all the time with stunning views to enjoy en route.*

character, with cafés lining the tiny crescent harbour where colourful fishing boats anchor.
*The easiest stretch of the walk: from Riomaggiore take the paved Via dell'Amore ('Road of Love') to Manarola, which passes through tunnels and follows the coast at sea level most of the way.*

## 2 Manarola

Sprawled over a rock, Manarola is one of the most atmospheric villages, with pastel buildings overlooking a shimmering harbour, while above the hamlet are terraces of grapes and olives. Shops sell locally produced olive oil and wine – you've probably walked right by the vineyards and groves they came from!
*Climb the stairs to Punto Bunofiglio, overlooking the sea. At the top, the views of Punta del Mesco and the coast ahead are stunning. Part of the walk is over disued railway tracks.*

## 3 Corniglia

Situated higher above the sea than the other villages, Corniglia is probably the most dramatically located of the villages; its sea views are spectacular in the early

## 4 Vernazza

Vernazza, with its tiny squares, elegant arcades and lovely *loggias*, is the most fairy-tale of the villages. The lemon-coloured Chiesa di Santa Margherita is splendidly set on the waterfront. Vernazza's fish restaurants make it a good spot for lunch.
*The next section of the trail is the most ruggedly beautiful part of the walk, taking around 1½ hours, and is the most demanding and rigorous of all. The vegetation is wild, sheer cliffs drop dramatically to the sea, and the trail is in poor condition in parts: take care on this stretch.*

## 5 Monterosso al Mare

With a pretty port, good beaches, dramatic cliffs and loads of restaurants and rooms to rent, Monterosso al Mare is the largest and busiest of the villages, and the choice of many travellers staying overnight. The old and 'new' centres of Monterosso al Mare are separated by the Hill of Cappuccini and connected by a tunnel.

## EMILIA-ROMAGNA
### Bologna

With beguiling medieval architecture, atmospheric arcades, Europe's oldest university and sublime cuisine, Bologna is simply captivating. Long known as an intellectual centre with a rich culture – the university was founded in 1088 – Bologna has a vibrant social life with buzzy bars and cafés, an eclectic offering of art exhibitions, concerts and performances, and a live music and jazz scene that's the envy of other cities.

A gastronomic capital, it boasts a bustling market with store after store crammed to the rafters with local specialities, from *mortadella* to fresh pasta. Devote a couple of hours to browsing the gourmet shops that line the narrow cobblestone lanes off the main square.

Bologna has one of Northern Italy's most architecturally unified historical centres, and one of the great delights here is simply relaxing in the piazzas, visiting the churches, strolling along the cobblestone streets and ambling under the elegant arcades of the city's sienna buildings. Start at **Piazza Maggiore** and **Piazza del Nattuno**, Bologna's connecting main squares in the historical centre, each lined with elegant

Imposing architecture in Piazza del Nattuno, Bologna

Renaissance and medieval architecture; its splendid 16th-century **Fontana di Nettuno** (Fountain of Neptune) is a popular local meeting place. The colossal Gothic 14th-century **Basilica di San Petronio** (*Piazza Maggiore. Tel: (051) 225442. Open: daily 7.30am–1pm & 2.30–6pm. Free admission*) features 22 chapels decorated with vibrant frescoes and splendid art.

Nearby, the 12th-century leaning towers, **Torre degli Asinelli** (Tower of the Asinelli) and **Torre Garisenda** (Garisenda Tower. *Piazza di Porta Ravegnana. Open: daily 9am–6pm. Admission charge*) are symbols of Bologna's affluence. Built by powerful families, the taller the tower, the more influential the dynasty. The 49m (161ft) Garisenda Tower, which had its top chopped off in the 14th century as it was considered in danger of falling, is inaccessible, while the taller 102m (335ft) Asinelli Tower boasts breathtaking views of Bologna's red-tiled roofs. From here, you can stroll down Via Strada Maggiore, an atmospheric street boasting block after block of colonnades, to the lively University Quarter, home to the University buildings.

Bologna is also home to some superb museums. The **Museo Civico Archeologico** (Archaeological Museum. *Via dell'Archiginnasio 2. Tel: (051) 275 72 11. Open: Tue–Fri 9am–3pm, Sat & Sun 10am–6pm. Closed: Mon. Admission charge*) houses an exceptional Egyptian collection of over 100,000 pieces, including myriad mummies and sarcophagi, as well as Roman and Greek

The leaning towers of Asinelli and Garisenda

sculptures and relics. Visit the tourist office (*Piazza Maggiore 1/e. Tel: (051) 239660. Open: daily 9am–7pm, until 5pm 31 Dec*) for their comprehensive *Bologna Pianta-Guida* (Guide-Map of Bologna; around €5) and *Guida ai Musei di Bologna* (Guide to the Museums of Bologna; free), also including map, and their boxed set of imaginatively themed walking tours.

Don't miss the 13th-century **Basilica di San Domenico** (Saint Dominic Basilica, *Piazza San Domenico 13. Tel: (051) 640 0411. Open: daily 9am–noon & 3–5.30pm. Free admission*), which houses exquisite Renaissance tombs, frescoes, sculptures and art, including Michelangelo's statue of San Procolo.

**Liguria and Emilia-Romagna**

## Ferrara

Surrounded by Renaissance walls and boasting a perfectly preserved castle, a striking cathedral and an endless number of elegant palaces, this UNESCO World Heritage-listed city on the Po di Volano, a tributary of the Po River, is one of Northern Italy's most beautiful cities. The birthplace of legendary filmmaker Michelangelo Antonioni, Ferrara has a youthful vibe, and the fact that it sees few tourists exploring its streets only adds to its allure.

Ferrara owes its splendour to the influential and often ruthless Este dynasty and a series of generous arts patrons who married exceedingly well,

### LOCAL FLAVOUR

Many of the signature dishes and ingredients of Italian cooking originate in Northern Italy – and there's nothing quite like tasting these delights in the cities or regions that first produced them. Typical treats that you can sample on your travels are Parma hams and parmesan cheese in Parma; *ragù alla Bolognese* (Bolognese sauce) and *mortadella* in Bologna; *Aceto Balsamico Tradizionale* (balsamic vinegar) in Modena; *pesto alla Genovese* (basil pesto) in Genova; *cotoletta Milanese* (veal cutlets), *Ossobucco* (braised veal shanks), *risotto alla Milanese* (slow-cooked rice with saffron threads) in Milan; white truffles in Alba; *Bresaola della Valtellina* (air-cured beef) in Valtellina; *polenta* (cornmeal) and *Panettone* (a 'Christmas' bread) in Lombardia; and, of course, Gorgonzola for Gorgonzola cheese.

Castello Estense

leading them to embellish their city with riches to flaunt their success, beginning with Duke Ercole I, whose fortunes and enthusiasm for the arts in the late 15th and early 16th centuries attracted artists from all over Europe, enabling the city to flourish as a cultural centre revered for its fine Renaissance painting, music and architecture. Ercole's son Alfonso I, who was married to Lucrezia Borgia, supported music especially, leading Ferrara to become a notable centre for the lute, while his son, Ercole II, who married the daughter of French king Louis XII, furnished the city with even more extravagant buildings. Alfonso II, married to the sister of Emperor Maximilian II, is credited with creating a city so creatively rich it was rivalled only by Venice.

Ferrara's cathedral looms over Piazza Cattedrale

In the centre of Ferrara, the Este dynasty's lofty 14th-century residence, **Castello Estense** (*Piazza Castello. Viale Cavour. Tel: (0532) 299 233. Open: 9.30am–5.30pm Tue–Sun. Closed: Mon. www.castelloestense.it. Admission charge*) rises above a moat and comes complete with four soaring towers and an imposing drawbridge. It now hosts the tourist office and temporary exhibitions, although the royal suites and grisly dungeon are also open, the latter a big draw because it was where Duke Nicolò III had his young second wife and his son beheaded for being lovers.

Ferrara's 12th-century Gothic-Romanesque **cathedral** (*Piazza Cattedrale. Tel: (0532) 207449. Open: daily 7.30am–noon & 3–6.30pm. Free admission*) took over 100 years to complete and features a tiered marble façade sporting intricate carvings, a pair of splendid lion statues guarding the entrance, and atmospheric colonnades. In the evening, locals spill into the piazza out front from the adjoining bar. The cafés diagonally opposite make a fine spot for taking in the elaborate church while refuelling on equally elaborate sundaes.

## Modena

Boasting Italy's highest income per capita, Modena, the home of Pavarotti, Maserati, Ferrari and balsamic vinegar, is one of the North's most prosperous and refined cities.

Initially established as a Roman garrison in the 2nd century BC on the Via Emilia trade route, Modena was made a duchy by the powerful Este family following Ferrara's fall to the Papal States at the end of the 16th century. The Este dynasty controlled the city, apart from a brief period of Napoleonic rule, until Italian unification in the 19th century. As a consequence, Modena's medieval centre is blessed with beautiful palaces, pretty squares and excellent museums overflowing with precious art.

**Galleria Estense** exhibits the Este's collection, with works by El Greco, Velázquez, Bernini, Veronese and Tintoretto (*Palazzo dei Musei, Piazza Sant'Agostino 48. Tel: (059) 439 57 11. Open: Tue–Sun 8.30am–7.30pm. Closed: Mon. Admission charge*).

One of Italy's finest Romanesque cathedrals, the splendid World Heritage-listed 12th-century **Duomo**, with its leaning 12th- to 14th-century campanile, is Modena's main attraction, with a stunning portico with pillars supported by carved lions, an enormous 13th-century Gothic rose window, a vaulted ceiling, and vibrant bas-reliefs depicting medieval agricultural themes and scenes from Genesis (*Corso Duomo. Open: daily 7am–12.30pm & 3.30–7pm. Free admission*).

Undoubtedly the highlight of Northern Italy for car enthusiasts, Formula One fans and design buffs is the brilliant car museum **Galleria Ferrari** (*Via Dino Ferrari 43, Maranello. Tel: (053) 694 32 04. Open: May–Sept 9.30am–7pm; Oct–Apr 9.30am–6pm. www.galleria.ferrari.com. Admission charge. Bus marked 'Maranello' from Via Bacchini bus station*). There are sleek exhibitions featuring the cars themselves, from antique Ferraris to the latest models, the world of Formula One, including a re-creation of a pit, trophies and memorabilia, and the life of the legendary Enzo Ferrari.

## Parma

Situated on the Roman trade route Via Emilia, Parma is also regarded as Italy's culinary capital and an opera mecca. The city first rose in prominence and influence as a duchy under the Farnese dynasty in the 16th century and continued its artistic ascension under Bourbon ruler Marie-Louise, Napoleon's second wife, and a generous patron of the arts. Marie-Louise commissioned the construction of Parma's famed opera house, Teatro Regio, where Verdi staged operas such as *Aida*.

The birthplace of Parmigianino, Toscanini, Bodoni, prosciutto and parmesan cheese, Parma boasts a beautifully preserved historical centre, exquisite art and architecture, and superb museums, including the **Musei**

Parma's cathedral, campanile and baptistery

**del Cibo** (Food Museums). These include an array of museums in the area dedicated to regional specialities and offer the chance to view their production and sample them. Museum hours vary and are limited. For details contact the tourist office (*Via Melloni 1. Tel: (0521) 218855. www.museidelcibo.it. Open: daily 9am–7pm*).

Other highlights include the imposing, pink 11th-century Romanesque **Duomo** with its pretty loggias, a porch guarded by lion statues, and a cupola richly decorated by Correggio with Renaissance frescoes (*Piazza del Duomo. Tel: (0521) 235886. Open: daily 9am–12.30pm & 3–7pm. Free admission*). Adjoining it is a remarkable Gothic-Romanesque **campanile** and pink Romanesque

**Battistero** (baptistery), featuring vivid frescoes of biblical scenes.

Marie-Louise's significant collection of art is on show at the **Galleria Nazionale** (National Gallery) (*Piazzale della Pilotta 15. Tel: (0521) 233309. www.gallerianazionaleparma.it. Open: Tue–Sun 8.30am–1.30pm. Closed: Mon. Admission charge*) in Palazzo della Pilotta, which also houses the **Museo Archeologico Nazionale** (National Archaeological Museum) (*Tel: (0521) 233718. Open: Oct–May Tue–Sat 9am–1pm, Sun 3–5pm; Jun–Sept Tue–Sat 9am–1pm, Sun 9.30am–12.30pm & 4–7pm. Closed: Mon*). The collection features work by Parma artists from the 15th to 19th centuries, including the great painter Correggio, whose masterpiece *Madonna with Saint Jerome* is on display.

# Supercar city

Modena is the spiritual home of the supercar. From the late 1940s when road cars began to reflect the features of cars on the racetrack, Modena was the touchstone. Even when cars from England (the sexy Jaguar E-Type) and from Germany (the brutal Porsche 911 Turbo) made a splash, Modena's Lamborghini, Ferrari and Maserati responded – and they never disappointed. Through oil crises, financial crises, takeovers and buyouts, what remains a constant in Modena is making beautiful machines that go fast.

A selection of Ferrari track cars

There is no greater name in making gorgeous cars than Ferrari. From its factory in nearby Maranello, some of the greatest cars in the world have rolled out the doors. Founded in 1929 by Enzo Ferrari, they produced racing cars exclusively until 1947 when the brand began producing barely disguised racing cars for the road. Crucial to the success of Ferrari has been its continual involvement – and overwhelming success – in Formula One racing. Desirable, fast and beautiful cars have been Maranello's trademark, and the Pininfarina-designed bodies, such as the Dino, Daytona, 308, F355 and 550 Maranello, are all-time classics (*see Designing Turin, p27*). Although Ferrari has been part of the Fiat empire since 1969, it's carried on doing what it does best, and the legendary F40, F50 and the 354km/h (220mph) Enzo that were launched in the 1980s, 1990s and 2000s respectively, as well as its Formula One success, prove this point.

Keeping Ferrari on its toes during the height of supercar madness was Maserati, started by six brothers early in the 20th century and making their first road car in 1926. A successful racing company, Maserati brought out the innovative Tipo 61 racing car in the

Formula One cars on display at Galleria Ferrari in Maranello

1960s, a model that also joined the club of mind-bogglingly fast road cars and could reach 285km/h (177mph). Maserati's Ghibli combined a top speed of over 250km/h (155mph) with a level of comfort that belied its wild speed. After many turbulent years, Fiat acquired Maserati in 1991, which became part of the Ferrari family in 1997, and focused on its best attributes – luxury and speed. The company separated from Ferrari in 2005 and is a successful luxury brand under the Fiat umbrella.

It was a disgruntled Ferrari owner who started another of Modena's sports car companies after Enzo Ferrari ignored his complaints. Tractor maker Ferruccio Lamborghini's first car, the 350 GT from 1963, was a hit, but it was the stunning Lamborghini Miura that was the breakthrough car in 1965. With the wonderful V12 engine mounted in the middle of the car for better balance – handy when the car does 270km/h (168mph) – it was considered the first true supercar. Other famous models followed; the Countach and the Diablo are legendary. Today, under the wing of German brand Audi, they haven't become too austere – their latest model, the Reventón, has a production run of just 20 and costs a cool one million euros.

And while many mourn the loss of the independent supercar maker, the Modena-based Pagani has had success with its first model, the Zonda, with designer Horacio Pagani hoping to usher in a new Renaissance of the supercar.

## Po Delta

The Po River, at 652km (405 miles) long, is Italy's longest. A bird-watcher's paradise, the pristine wetlands of its delta are a picturesque UNESCO World Heritage-listed nature reserve that stretches inland along the coast between Ferrara and Ravenna.

Comprised of marshes, lagoons, rivers, canals and floodplains, the natural wetlands are the largest in Italy, and are home to an abundance of bird species, including the grey heron, little egret, common snipe, great crested grebes, goosanders, sandpipers, black-headed gulls, Caspian gulls and great cormorants.

The best area for bird-watching is along the banks of the River Reno in the southern part of the Valli di Comacchio, while the best periods are the spring and autumn. Although not nearly as popular for fishing as it once was, the basin is nevertheless home to carp, perch, bass, catfish and eel.

Within the delta, Il Gran Bosco della Mesola (the Great Mesola Woods) boasts 1,000ha (2,471 acres) of dense forest of poplars, bay oaks, alders, hornbeams and junipers, and is home to deer, foxes, weasels, hares, turtles and tortoises. There are paths through the woods that are wonderful for walks and bike rides.

For those who aren't into bird-watching, the diminutive town of Comacchio is worth a quick stop. There are a couple of pretty bridges that cross

The red-brick façade of the Basilica di San Vitale in Ravenna

a canal, and a pleasant waterside square. The town is famous for its local cuisine based on eel, and a number of *trattorie* serve an array of eel specialities, including eel risotto and stewed eel served with polenta, a must-try for adventurous foodies.

## Ravenna

With World Heritage-listed architecture, imposing churches, and an astonishing array of Byzantine mosaics scattered around the town, Ravenna is a compelling place to spend a couple of days.

The town has been the capital of three great empires, the Western Roman Empire from AD 402, the Visigoth Empire from AD 473, and the Byzantine Empire from AD 540–752, and the Byzantines can be thanked for Ravenna's key attractions – beautifully preserved mosaics that were created between the 6th and 8th centuries, when the empire flourished here.

They can be appreciated at several locations spread around the compact centre. The octagonal-domed 6th-century **Basilica di San Vitale** (*Via San Vitale 17. Tel: (0544) 215193. Open: Apr–Sept 9am–7pm, Mar & Oct 9am–5.30pm, Nov–Feb 9.30am–4.30pm. Admission charge*) boasts gorgeous green and gold mosaics, including one of a beardless Christ and angels, and splendid mosaics of Emperor Justinian and Empress Theodora. The fairly new **Domus dei Tappeti di Pietra** (*House of Stone Carpets; Chiesa di San Eufemia,Via Barbiani. Tel: (0544) 32512. www.domusdeitappetidipietra.it. Open: Mar–Oct daily 10am–6.30pm; Nov–Feb Tue–Fri 10am–5pm, Sat & Sun 10am–6pm. Closed: Mon. Admission charge*) features floor after floor of stunning mosaics, while there are some fascinating ones in the Cappella di San Andrea (Saint Andrew Chapel) at the **Museo Arcivescovile** (Archepiscopal Museum) (*Piazza Arcivescovado. Tel: (0544) 215201. Open: daily Apr–Sept 9am–7pm; Mar & Oct 9am–5.30pm; Nov–Feb 9.30am–4.30pm. Admission charge*). These intriguing mosaics feature Christ in armour treading on a lion's head, angels and busts of saints. The pride and joy of the museum is an elaborate ivory throne dating back to the 6th century, which was carved for Archbishop Maximianus of Constantinople.

There are more splendid remnants of the Byzantine period at the **Museo Nazionale di Ravenna** (National Museum of Ravenna) (*Via Fiandrini. Tel: (0544) 344 24. Open: Tue–Sun 8.30am–7.30pm. Closed: Mon. Admission charge*), which is home to an array of icons, tapestries, ceramics and weapons.

The tourist office (*Via Salara 8. Tel: (0544) 35404. www.turismo.ravenna.it. Open: Mon–Sat 8.30am–6pm, Sun 10am–4pm*) is one of the region's more helpful ones with good maps and information, a discount card that gives entry to myriad city sights, and free bikes to ride.

# Lombardia

*Bounded by the colossal Swiss Alps to the north, and the provinces of Piemonte to the west, Emilia-Romagna to the south and Veneto to the east, Lombardia is Italy's most densely populated and industrialised region. Yet it's still surprisingly lovely and extremely liveable, especially its elegant, medieval cities, such as beautiful hilltop Bergamo, the violin-making centre of Cremona, the laid-back and oft-overlooked Mantova, and the picturesque lakes area.*

The lakes area takes in massive Lago Maggiore, which flows along River Ticino into the River Po, with pretty Verbania and Stresa on its shores; delightful, diminutive Lago d'Orta, the most intimate and exclusive of the lakes, with quaint Orta San Giulio; refined Lago di Como, the elegant town of Como and the enchanting villages of Bellagio and Varenna; and family-oriented Lago di Garda with its theme parks, thermal spas and watersports. All of the lakes boast grand old hotels, charming cobblestone villages, and gracious lakeside villas with bougainvillea-filled gardens.

Then there's the stylish regional capital of Milan at the region's heart, also Italy's economic capital and Northern Italy's wealthiest city, with a population second in size only to Rome's. An art, food and fashion capital, Milan is a rewarding city for those who take time to explore it.

## Milan

Chic and sophisticated, Italy's fashion capital (if not the world's) has much to offer visitors, from its magnificent cathedral, one of the country's most beautiful, to its array of superb museums and art, of which Leonardo da Vinci's *The Last Supper* is the standout.

Inhabited for 70,000 years, Milan was founded in the 7th century BC and inhabited by Gallo-Celtic tribes until the Romans arrived in 222 BC. They named it Mediolanum and it prospered due to its strategic location on trade

### APERITIVO HOUR

No one's sure where the notion of the aperitif came from, but since 1786, when vermouth was invented in Turin, Italians have enjoyed a pre-dinner drink. The aperitif, or *aperitivo* in Italian, came from the Latin 'to open', seeing an alcoholic pre-dinner drink as something to 'open the stomach'. While drinks are generally slightly cheaper during *aperitivo* time, it's not treated like 'happy hour' where you imbibe as much as possible in the allotted time. In Milan it's more about catching up with friends after work, relaxing, and snacking on the spreads of finger food that come with the ritual. While the scene is biggest in Milan, it's also popular in Turin, Genova and Parma.

Lombardia

routes between Rome and Northern Europe. In 15 BC Emperor Augustus made the settlement the regional capital. When the Roman Empire adopted Christianity in AD 313, many fine churches were built; this was when the Bishop of Mediolanum, Ambrose, commissioned the splendid Basilica di Sant'Ambrogio. With the Roman Empire's decline in AD 402, Milan lost its influence and in 569 was conquered by the Lombards.

After a *comune* (town council) and city-state were formed in the 11th century Milan grew rapidly, until its occupation by Holy Roman emperor Barbarossa (Frederick I) in 1162. In 1176 Milan's key families and allies formed the *Lega Lombarda* and from the 13th century the city was governed by a succession of dynasties, the most important being the Viscontis (1262–1447) and the Sforza (1450–1535), responsible for Milan's flourishing.

You don't have to be a fashionista to appreciate Milan, but if you didn't pay attention to style before, you will now. Milan oozes it: from its fine design products to the Milanese women who look elegant riding motor scooters (in high heels!) and the city's teenagers who would win any best-dressed teen awards.

However, Milan is also a city with substance and is surprisingly down-to-earth. The Milanese are hard-working and smart and are lovers of literature, art and – of course – opera.

Strolling the streets in Milan is a relaxed affair compared to London and Paris, and no neighbourhood epitomises that laid-back attitude better than the Navigli where it's all about enjoying an *aperitivo* with friends, leisurely dining at a *trattoria*, strolling along the canals with a *gelato*, and watching a jazz band perform on the cobblestone streets outside a café.

**Castello Sforzesco (Sforzesco Castle)**
Built by Galeazzo II Visconti in 1368, the colossal red-brick Castello Sforzesco was remodelled in the 15th century by Francesco Sforza with Leonardo da Vinci's help. It's now home to superb museums including **Museo Egizio** (Egyptian Museum) with a fascinating collection of mummies; the **Pinacoteca** (Art Gallery, *see p75*), covering medieval times through to the 18th century; **Museo d'Arte Antica** (Museum of Antiquities), boasting Lombard sculptures, a da Vinci fresco, and Michelangelo's unfinished *Rondanini Pietà*; and **Museo degli Strumenti Musicali**, one of Europe's largest musical instrument museums, featuring rare violins by Stradivarius. *Piazza Castello. Tel: (02) 8846 3700. www.milanocastello.it. Open: daily 9am–5.30pm. Admission charge. Metro: Cairoli.*

Clock on the wall of Castello Sforzesco

## *Il Cenacolo* (The Last Supper)

Leonardo da Vinci's magnificent mural is Milan's most visited attraction. Decorating one wall of *Cenacolo Vinciano*, the refectory at Chiesa di Santa Maria delle Grazie, the mural was painted between 1495 and 1498. Over the years, the painting has been so damaged by floods, bombs and bad restoration that it is amazing that it has survived at all. Reserve your tickets in advance online (*www.cenacolovinciano.it*) or by phone and be there 15 minutes ahead of time or risk losing your place.

*Piazza Santa Maria delle Grazie 2, Corso Magenta. Tel: (02) 8942 1146. Open: Tue–Sun 8am–7.30pm. Closed: Mon. Admission charge. Metro: Cadorna.*

## Basilica di Sant'Ambrogio (Basilica of Saint Ambrose)

Built by Bishop Ambrogio (Ambrose), the patron saint of Milan, between AD 379 and 386, this unusual basilica has been rebuilt and restored several times, explaining its medley of styles. Notable are the two striking bell towers and inside a 9th-century altar depicting Jesus' life on the front and Saint Ambrose's on the back. It houses the remains of the saint.

*Piazza Sant'Ambrogio 15. Tel: (02) 8645 0895. www.santambrogio-basilica.it. Open: daily 9am–noon & 2–7pm. Metro: Sant'Ambrogio.*

## Duomo (Cathedral)

Commissioned in 1386 by Gian Galeazzo Visconti, Milan's Duomo holds 40,000 worshippers and measures 158m (518ft) long and 33m (108ft) wide, making it Italy's largest Gothic structure and one of the world's biggest cathedrals. While the size is astonishing, it's the intricate details, elaborate statues (some 2,000!), pretty spires (135!), decorative pillars and flying buttresses that are more impressive. Canals were dredged to carry the marble from quarries in Lago Maggiore to Milan. Inside, there are five aisles, 52 huge pillars, splendid 15th-century stained-glass windows, and some intriguing tombs. Visit in the morning or late afternoon when the light is best for the rooftop (accessed by stairs or elevator).

*Piazza del Duomo. www.duomomilano.it. Open: Cathedral 7am–7pm; rooftop 9am–5.45pm. Free admission to cathedral, admission charge for museum and rooftop. Metro: Duomo.*

### REDOING MILAN'S DUOMO

Although the first bricks of the cathedral were laid in 1386, it's incredibly still not *really* finished. Inaugurated in 1965, some of the detailed statues are still not completed and some stained glass is still to be put in place. While the brilliant façade was finished in 1813, it has been under wraps since 2002, when a thorough cleaning and restoration programme began. There is one saving grace: even though several architectural periods passed during the building of the great cathedral, it still retains its Gothic splendour.

The ornate interior of the museum inside Teatro alla Scala

### Galleria Vittorio Emanuele II

Milan's most prestigious shopping arcade, the *Galleria* was named after Italy's first king, although it was originally dedicated to Austria's Emperor Franz Joseph when the project was initiated in 1859. Designed by Giuseppe Mengoni, the spectacular gallery was built between 1864 and 1878, and was one of Europe's first buildings to use iron and glass as structural elements. Practically destroyed by World War II bombing, it was rebuilt during the post-war period. *Galleria Vittorio Emanuele II, Piazza del Duomo. Open: daily, 24 hours. Free admission. Metro: Duomo.*

### Museo Poldi Pezzoli (Poldi Pezzoli Museum)

In 1850 passionate art collector Poldi Pezzoli employed some of the most innovative artists of the time to decorate his apartments in the family *palazzo*. Each room was decorated in a different style. Sadly, the *palazzo* was destroyed during World War II bombing raids; however, its precious collection had been safely hidden away. Reconstructed and opened to the public in 1951, it has remained one of Milan's finest house-museums ever since.
*Via Manzoni 12. Tel: (02) 796 334. www.museopoldipezzoli.it. Open: Tue–Sun 10am–6pm. Closed: Mon. Admission charge. Metro: Montenapoleone.*

### Pinacoteca di Brera (Brera Art Gallery)

Home to one of Italy's most important art collections, the Pinacoteca di Brera is a must for art lovers. Housed in the magnificent 17th-century Palazzo di Brera, the extensive collection contains pieces from the 13th to 20th centuries, including outstanding works by Mantegna, Raphael, Bellini, Caravaggio

and Tiepolo, along with work by Goya, Rembrandt, El Greco and Picasso.
*Palazzo di Brera, Via Brera 28.*
*Tel: (02) 722 631.*
*www.brera.beniculturali.it.*
*Open: Tue–Sun 8.30am–7.15pm.*
*Closed: Mon. Admission charge. Metro:*
*Montenapoleone.*

## Quadrilatero d'Oro
## (The Golden Quarter)

Milan's famous fashion district, the cobblestone streets of this glamorous area are home to the headquarters and flagship stores of Chanel, Dolce&Gabbana, Gucci, Missoni, Prada and Versace, among others.
*Between Via della Spiga, Via Sant'Andrea, Via Monte Napoleone & Via Alessandro Manzoni. Shops open: Mon–Sat 10am–7pm. Metro: Montenapoleone.*

Stained glass at Museo Poldi Pezzoli

Lombardia

### LA SCALA SOAP OPERA

As if the operas staged at this renowned opera house didn't have enough drama, Puccini or Verdi could have written the story of the restoration of Teatro alla Scala. After the season opening in 2001, the opera moved to a new theatre in an industrial part of town – much to the displeasure of opera fans. Also displeasing to fans was the theatre restoration and the addition of a 'fly tower' allowing sets to be stored more efficiently. All was forgiven after the successful reopening in 2004, but the long-time theatre manager was fired in 2005, leading to a no-confidence vote in the conductor by the orchestra and other staff, forcing the conductor to resign.

### Teatro alla Scala

The plush, gilt-edged interior of Milan's elegant opera house was inaugurated in 1778 with Salieri's opera *Europa Riconsciuta* and ever since has hosted many memorable first nights, from Vincenzo Bellini's masterpiece *Norma* in 1831, reviled by the Milanese, to Puccini's 1904 *Madama Butterfly* premiere, which failed to please its audience. Destroyed by World War II bombs, it reopened in 1946 after extensive rebuilding, and in recent years has undegone further renovations (*see box above*). A night at an opera is a must. Also visit the theatre's excellent museum. The informative tours enable you to visit the theatre.
*Piazza della Scala, Via Filodrammatici 2.*
*Tel: (02) 88791 and (02) 7200 3744*
*(Infotel, Ticket Information).*
*www.teatroallascala.org. Museum open:*
*daily 9am–12.30pm & 1.30–5.30pm.*
*Metro: Duomo.*

# Walk: Milan city centre

*The brisk walk along Milan's chic cobblestone streets takes in the city's main attractions, from its massive main square, Piazza del Duomo, and the imposing cathedral itself, to the arty Brera area, along the way visiting several of the city's finest museums, before finishing in time for an aperitivo down at Milan's liveliest neighbourhood, Navigli.*

*Allow two hours for the walk only, eight including museum visits.*

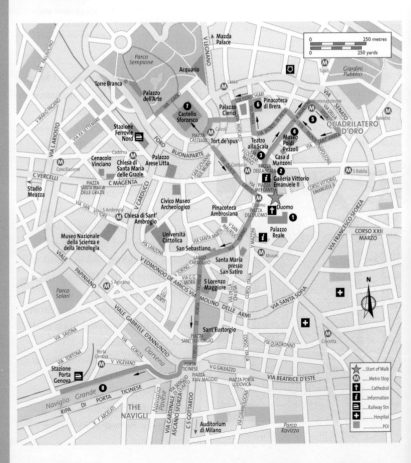

## 1 Duomo

Admire the Duomo's impressive interior before visiting its rooftop for great views of Milan, and the chance to get a close look at the extraordinary statues, including the gold *Madonnina* ('little Madonna') atop the central spire.
*Cross Piazza del Duomo to Galleria Vittorio Emanuele II.*

## 2 Galleria Vittorio Emanuele II

Stroll this elegant shopping arcade, stopping under the central 47m (154ft) high glass dome to admire the ceiling and floor mosaics. Rub your foot across Taurus the Bull's testicles for good luck – it's a local custom!
*Exit on Piazza della Scala.*

## 3 Teatro alla Scala

Visit the theatre's fabulous museum, home to fascinating displays of costumes, instruments, opera glasses and performance mementoes.
*Follow Via Alessandro Manzoni.*

## 4 Museo Poldi Pezzoli

*See p72.*
*Follow Via Alessandro Manzoni, turning right on Via della Spiga, then right on Via Sant'Andrea.*

## 5 Quadrilatero d'Oro

Even if you're not a fashionista, the elegant cobblestone streets of the fashion district are worth exploring to admire the elegant neoclassical architecture and jaw-dropping window displays (especially fabulous at night).

*Turn right into Via Monte Napoleone, following it to Via Alessandro Manzoni. Cross the road and follow Via Monte di Pieta, turning right on Via Brera.*

## 6 Pinacoteca di Brera

The charming streets of arty Brera are lined with art galleries, antique shops and cafés, but the quarter is most famously home to the impressive Pinacoteca di Brera, which you can visit.
*Turn left onto Via Fiori Chiari. At the end turn left and at Via Sacchi turn right to Foro Buonaparte, crossing to the castle.*

## 7 Castello Sforzesco

Enjoy an array of superlative museums, then stroll behind the castle to leafy Parco Sempione, a sprawling 47ha (116-acre) park featuring a splendid neoclassical arch and Torre Branca, a 103m (338ft) tall steel tower.
*From the castle cross Foro Buonaparte and follow Via Dante across Piazza Cordusio to Via Orefici. Turn right onto Via Torino, veer left onto Corso di Porta Ticinese, then cross Porta Ticinese, turning right onto Via Gorizia and left onto pedestrian-only Naviglio Grande.*

## 8 Navigli

*Naviglio* means canal in Italian and the *Naviglio Grande* (Big Canal), built in the 13th century, was Milan's first navigable man-made waterway, rapidly becoming an important trade route. Now lined with cafés, pizzerias, *trattorie* and *enoteche*, it's Milan's liveliest neighbourhood.

## Bergamo

The beautiful medieval city of
Bergamo, at the foothills of the Alps, is
divided into two towns: an enchanting,
walled, medieval upper town, the
*città alta*, which is surrounded by a
sprawling, elegant lower town, the *città
bassa*. While the lower town, with its
wide boulevards, grand buildings and
buzzy cafés, has much to offer, visitors
tend to spend most if not all of their
time in the upper town.

Like many Northern Italian cities,
Bergamo has experienced long periods
of domination by outsiders, and as
a result of this continued cultural
resistance possesses a strong identity,
evidenced in the incomprehensible
local dialect you'll hear on its hilly
cobblestone lanes, and its rich cuisine.

Begin in the upper town, accessible
by a 120-year-old *funicolare* (funicular),
and easily explored on foot. While it's a
pleasure simply to stroll the pedestrian

Piazza Vecchia, with Torre Civica in the background

Lombardia

streets, browse the charming shops and linger in the cafés and bars, Bergamo boasts a wealth of cultural and artistic treasures that demand your attention, and there are a few not to be missed.

From the funicular, follow Via Gombito to the attractive 15th-century **Piazza Vecchia** (Old Square). The administrative heart of Bergamo for centuries, and boasting beautiful medieval and Renaissance architecture, aristocratic *palazzi* and a splendid Venetian fountain, this is also the social heart of the lively town, lined with cafés and restaurants. The stone 12th-century **Palazzo della Ragione** (being renovated and under scaffolding at the time of research) with its loggia is the prettiest here, while the 12th-century **Campanone** or **Torre Civica** (Civic Bell Tower. *Piazza Vecchia. Tel: (035) 247 116. Open: Tue–Sun 9.30am–7pm. Closed: Mon. Admission charge*) has spectacular views of the old town and surrounds.

Beyond Piazza Vecchia on Piazza del Duomo are Bergamo's three highlights, the colossal red-brick **Basilica Santa Maria Maggiore**, the white marble **Duomo** (whose façade was also under restoration at the time of research), the ornate **Cappella Colleoni** (Colleoni Chapel), and on the fourth side on the square, the pretty apricot marble **Battistero** (Baptistry).

If you continue along Via Gombito, which becomes Via Colleoni, you'll arrive at Piazza della Cittadella, a square that is mostly now used as a car

Cappella Colleoni

park, but which is home to two small but worthwhile museums, the **Museo Archeologico** (Archaeological Museum. *Piazza Cittadella 9. Tel: (035) 242 839*) and the **Museo Scienze Naturali** (Museum of Natural History. *Piazza Cittadella 10. Email: infomuseoscienze@comune.bg.it*).

If you only have time for one museum, however, head down to the lower town and choose between either the **Accademia Carrara** (Carrara Academy. *Piazza Carrara 82. Tel: (035) 247 149. www.accademiacarrara.bergamo.it. Open: daily 10am–5.30pm. Admission charge*), home to one of Northern Italy's richest collections of medieval, Renaissance and Baroque art, or GAMEC, the **Galleria d'Arte Moderna e Contemporanea** (*Via San Tomaso 53. Tel: (035) 270 272. www.gamec.it*), Bergamo's brilliant gallery of modern and contemporary art, which has an excellent permanent collection as well as hosting engaging and often provocative temporary exhibitions.

## Cremona

Famously known as the home of violin-making and specifically the celebrated Stradivari violin, this compact and sophisticated town is a must-visit for music lovers, who should make a beeline for the outstanding **Museo Stradivariano** (*Via Ugolani Dati. Tel: (0372) 407 269. Open: Tue–Sun 9am–6pm. Admission charge*), in the Museo Civica Ala Ponzone, and the **Palazzo Comunale** (*Piazza del Comune 8. Tel: (0372) 407 033. Open: Mon–Sat 9am–6pm, Sun 10am–6pm. Admission charge*) to see the Collezione Gli Archi, a small but significant collection of instruments.

The Duomo in Cremona at night

The most revered violin makers learned their craft in Cremona, including Amati, Guarneri and Stradivari, and the city's reputation as the creator of the perfect violin is centuries old and as strong as ever. The city oozes music. Wander around the charming streets and you'll see signs for violin makers on workshop doors, often accessed from quaint courtyards, and you'll hear violins being tuned or practised.

Cremona is also famous for its monumental 12th-century cathedral, **Cattedrale di Santa Maria Assunta**, which dominates the main square and can be seen from far and wide, and for making fine-quality nougat.

For everyone else, Cremona has enough atmosphere and style, several superb museums, and in summer a lively nightlife, to warrant a day or two spent here.

## Lago di Como

Shaped like an upside-down 'Y', Lago di Como is Italy's third-largest lake, at 146sq km (56sq miles), after lakes Garda and Maggiore. It takes a full day to drive around the lake if you leave early in the morning; however, you could easily spend a week exploring it if you stopped off at villages along the way, and did boat trips and garden walks. At over 400m (1,310ft) deep, it's one of Europe's deepest lakes, which accounts for its cobalt colour.

Lago di Como has long been a popular destination among cultured

The garden of Villa Carlotta

travellers, and was popular with the Grand Tourists in the 19th century, when the lake's fans included Stendhal, Franz Liszt and Shelley. It is most famous for its gracious lakeside villas with their lush manicured lawns and graceful tropical gardens. Some of them, such as Villa Carlotta at Tremezzo, Villa del Balbianello and Villa d'Este at Cernobbio, are open to the public.

Built in 1690 for the Milanese marchese Giorgio Clerici, the lovely **Villa Carlotta** boasts a Romantic landscaped Italian garden, with symmetrical steps, pretty fountains and splendid sculptures. It was named after the daughter of Princess Marianne of Nassau to whom her mother gave the villa as a wedding gift. It was Carlotta and her husband, George II of Saxen-Meiningen, who developed the gardens. The villa itself is now a house-museum with some rooms dedicated to sculpture and art, and others furnished in the original period style.

Also famous for its ornate gardens is the former home of Italian explorer Guido Monzino, **Villa del Balbianello**, built in 1787.

Now a luxury hotel, the colossal **Villa d'Este**, built in 1568, boasts English-style gardens, while another hotel, **Villa Serbelloni** at Bellagio, more charming and intimate in comparison, backs onto a pretty 18th-century park.

There are many wonderful walks in the area, such as the 'Greenway del Lago di Como', a 10.5km (6½-mile) itinerary from Colonno to Cadenabbia di Griante that enables you to enjoy villas, gardens, Roman ruins and spectacular vistas on the way.

Like the other lakes, Lago di Como is also a popular spot for windsurfing, kitesurfing, sailing and swimming, although in recent years there have been fears that it was too polluted for swimming.

## Bellagio

Beguiling Bellagio is approached by car ferry from Menaggio and the views of the town from the boat are simply breathtaking. In an enchanting location at the tip of the peninsula, it also boasts its own jaw-dropping vistas of Lago di Como itself.

*30km (18¹/₂ miles) north of Como.*

## Como

With its grand hotels, excellent restaurants, waterfront bars and *gelaterie*, the elegant lakeside town of Como makes a fantastic starting point for boat cruises, drives and walks around the lake. The town itself is a fabulous place to explore, with its winding cobblestone lanes lined with chic shops, good museums and some fine churches.

The stunning **Duomo**, dating back to 1396, was built on the Romanesque Chiesa di Santa Maria Maggiore. Its splendid façade, not built until 1457, features an impressive portal guarded by two Renaissance statues of Pliny the Elder and Pliny the Younger, both famous locals from Como, a pretty rose window, and, inside, a decorated Rococo dome, a magnificently carved 16th-century choir, and marvellous tapestries and paintings dating to the 16th and 17th centuries.

A short stroll away, the Romanesque **Chiesa di San Fedele**, built in 1120, is famous for its intricately carved

Bellagio looks especially beautiful from the water

medieval door, while the 14th-century **Chiesa di Sant'Agostino** has a beautiful Baroque frescoed interior and graceful cloister.

Como also boasts some superb museums, including the **Museo Archeologico** (Archaeological Museum), **Museo Storico** (Historical Museum), the **Pinacoteca** (Art Gallery) and **Villa Olmo**, a splendid location for temporary exhibitions. During the summer months Como's piazzas, villas and gardens play host to a full programme of opera, classical music, jazz and world music concerts, most held under the stars.

## Lago di Garda

Italy's largest lake, this is nevertheless probably the least attractive of all of Italy's northern lakes, which says more about the splendour of the other lakes than it does about this lovely lake.

Very family-oriented, it's home to half a dozen theme parks, including Italy's version of Disneyland called Gardaland, amusement parks, waterparks and zoos. It's also more sports-oriented than the other lakes, with extensive watersports facilities and thermal spas. Windsurfing, kitesurfing, sailing, boating and fishing are all extremely popular here. While less refined than Lago di Como, Garda still has its fair share of alluring islands (including Isola del Garda, Isola San Biagio, Isola dell'Olivo, Isola di Sogno and Isola di Trimelone) and appealing towns and villages, such as Sirmione, Salo and Gardone Riviera.

Inside Como's Duomo

### Salò and Gardone Riviera

Salò and Gardone Riviera, tranquil and charming, are home to some grand luxurious hotels and attract a more mature, well-heeled traveller. Salò was a stronghold of the Milanese Visconti family but was known more as being the controversial capital of Mussolini's Nazi puppet state, the Republic of Salò, from 1943 to 1945. Now it's a quiet and picturesque village, as is nearby Gardone Riviera, which is also the address of the Vittoriale degli Italiani (the Shrine of Italian Victories), the weird and whimsical former residence of fascist poet Gabriele d'Annunzio. Its gardens are home to a military ship and the plane d'Annunzio used during raids on Vienna.

Scaliger Castle is a fine 13th-century building

### Sirmione

On a tiny peninsula jutting into the southern part of the lake, the picturesque walled town of Sirmione has a splendid castle, Il Castello di Sirmione la Rocca Scaligera (Scaliger Castle. *Tel: (030) 916 468. Open: Mar–mid-Oct 8.30am–7pm, mid-Oct–Feb 8.30am–5pm*), with drawbridges that cross a moat, and the ruins of a Roman spa, the Grotte di Catullo (Grotto of Catullus). The town is one of Lago di Garda's most popular attractions and as a result gets very crowded in summer.

### Lago Maggiore

The second largest of Italy's northern lakes after Garda, at an area of 215sq km (83sq miles), Lago Maggiore is the most westerly of the three enormous lakes. More dramatic in appearance than the more serene Lago di Como, Maggiore boasts craggy rocks, a temperate Mediterranean climate, the attractive pastel-painted towns of Verbania and Stresa, and an enchanting archipelago of garden-covered islands, including the breathtakingly beautiful Borromean Islands (*Isole Borromee*).

Located near the western shore of the lake, between Verbania and Stresa, the islands are owned by the Borromeo family, which started to buy them up in the 16th century (the first was Isola Madre) and still owns some of them to this day (Isola Madre, Isola Bella and Isola San Giovanni).

Named after Isabella the Countess Borromeo, **Isola Bella**, with its summer palace and terraces of gardens, is perhaps the loveliest. The largest, **Isola Madre**, boasts the most stunning gardens, English in style, and a richly decorated palace filled with art and antiques. **Isola Superiore**, also known as Isola dei Pescatori (the island of fishermen), named after the tiny fishing village on the island, is equally pretty.

**Verbania** and **Stresa** are the most attractive and most popular towns on the lake, both with a long history of tourism. Stresa was a hotspot in the 19th century, popular with European aristocrats who established enormous holiday villas here. Ernest Hemingway visited in 1948, and so charmed was he that he set part of his book *Farewell to Arms* in the Grand Hôtel des Îles Borromées.

Both towns boast delightful piazzas, pastel-coloured buildings and picturesque waterfronts with scenic walks. Stresa has a number of villas that can be visited, including the 18th-century **Villa Ducale**, **Villa Pallavicino**, now a zoological park, and **Villa Dell'Orto**, built in 1900 and designed by Boffi. Verbania is famous for its equally stunning **Villa Taranto** with its luxuriant Giardini Botanici (botanical gardens). Be warned, the towns are still immensely popular and hence very touristy, so prepare for crowds in summer.

## Lago d'Orta

Easily the most easy-going and enchanting of Italy's lakes, tranquil Lago d'Orta lies just west of Lago Maggiore. Less developed than the other lakes, with elegant aristocratic villas and wooded hills surrounding the lake, it has an air of intimacy and exclusivity that the other lakes don't possess.

A chartered boat on Lago d'Orta

The lake's main attraction is charming little **Orta San Giulio** and just offshore the captivating **Isola di San Giulio** (San Giulio Island). The lake itself was also once called Lago di San Giulio, after the 4th-century Saint Julius of Novara, the bishop who built the church and patron saint of the area.

Orta San Giulio is a tiny village of cobblestone lanes lined with pastel-coloured buildings housing delightful little stores, gourmet grocery shops and wine bars. There's a pretty leafy square, surrounded by terrace cafés, and a shady seaside promenade with park benches. Isola di San Giulio itself is worth a short excursion and boats cruise across frequently.

Just 275m (300yds) long from north to south and 140m (155yds) wide from east to west, Isola di San Giulio is home to the Basilica of Saint Giulio. Don't miss **Villa Crespi**, a magical Moorish-style boutique hotel and Michelin-starred restaurant just outside the village. At the northern end of the lake, **Omegna**, with a picturesque canal, is also worth visiting and is a fine spot to stop for lunch if you're doing a circuit of the lake.

## Mantova

Spectacularly sited on a small peninsula jutting into artificial lakes, created in the 12th century for defensive purposes, this small city is rather special. Yet it is surprisingly overlooked as a destination by most tourists, which means when all the other northern Italian cities are uncomfortably crowded in summer, Mantova has only a smattering of visitors, making it a wonderful place to spend a couple of relaxing days.

Mantova's massive Palazzo Ducale

The city boasts an impressive castle that is actually a complex of several regal buildings that make up the **Palazzo Ducale** (*Piazza Giovanni Paccagnini 3. Tel: (0376) 352 111*), the residence of the Gonzaga family. It includes the **Palazzo del Capitano**, the **Castello di San Giorgio** (Castle of Saint George) and the **Magna Domus**, and within these are leafy gardens and courtyards. These buildings preside over a striking square lined with cafés, an austere but enormous **Duomo** (*Piazza Sordello*), and dozens of splendid palaces, many built during the Austrian Habsburgs' rule, such as the Renaissance-style **Palazzo Te** (1525–35). The commercial centre's elegant arcades are home to sophisticated shops and the city has no shortage of restaurants.

## Pavia

Not far south from Milan and now known mainly for its agriculture and industry, Pavia was once Northern Italy's most powerful city. While it has a charming medieval centre and some lovely sights, including the **Università di Pavia**, one of Europe's oldest universities, it's most famous for the Certosa di Pavia (*see below*).

### Certosa di Pavia (Charterhouse of Pavia)

The breathtakingly beautiful charterhouse is a fairytale Carthusian monastery complex, built between 1396 and 1465, and located in the leafy emerald grounds that were once the

Certosa di Pavia

hunting park of Milan's Visconti dynasty. The Carthusian monastic order was founded in 1044 by Saint Bruno at Chartreuse, France (you can buy some of their famous Chartreuse liqueur here), and there is also a splendid monastery in Serra San Bruno in Calabria. But neither can compete with Pavia's Certosa in terms of the splendour of the Gothic and Renaissance architecture here.

Commissioned by Gian Galeazzo Visconti and intended to hold the Visconti family mausoleum, the church and monastery are grand in design, exuberant in style, and hold a rich collection of art. A visit here is a feast for the eyes, so allow plenty of time. It's possible to stroll around the tranquil cloisters, from where there is a spectacular view of the church exterior. *8km (5 miles) north of Pavia.*

# Veneto and Friuli-Venezia Giulia

*When visitors to Italy think of the Veneto region, they immediately think of Venice, a city that dazzles as much as it disappoints. Yet a day trip away are a handful of cities and towns that are some of Northern Italy's most delightful – from diminutive Padova to romantic Verona – while adjoining Veneto is the fascinating Friuli-Venezia Giulia region with its Central European flavour and elegant capital Trieste.*

Situated in northeastern Italy at the top of the boot, Veneto borders the regions of Trentino-Alto Adige and Lombardia in the west, Emilia-Romagna to the south, Austria in the northeast and Friuli-Venezia Giulia in the east, which in turn borders Slovenia in the east and Austria in the north, while its southern shore is lapped by the Adriatic Sea.

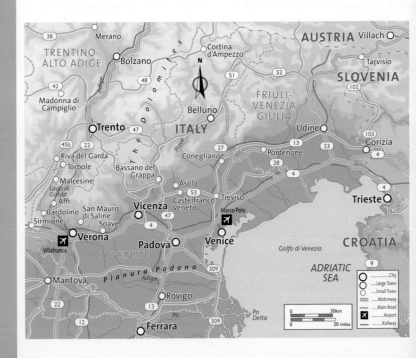

One of Italy's richest regions both culturally and financially, Veneto's main industry is tourism, so naturally there's an abundance of things to see and do. While they might be small regions, Veneto and Friuli-Venezia Giulia boast some of Northern Italy's most spectacular and varied landscapes, from the dramatic mountains, pretty valleys and striking rock formations of the Alps and Dolomites, to the Po Valley's sprawling flat plains and marshes rich with wildlife, Lago di Garda's alluring eastern shores and the Adriatic Sea's pine-backed beaches.

The regions boast two of Italy's most intriguing histories. Settled since the 2nd millennium BC by the Euganei and then the Veneti from Asia Minor, the regions' inhabitants developed trade with the Etruscans and Greeks and by the 4th century BC the society was prosperous with a sophisticated culture and language, Venetic. Fighting alongside the Romans against Hannibal and the Carthaginians, the Veneti were granted full Roman citizenship in 49 BC until the Roman Civil War in 42 BC, when, along with Friuli, they became part of the larger empire of Italia. Patavium (Padova), meanwhile, adopted Latin and became a *Pax Romana* city, with Tarvisium (Treviso) and Vicetia (Vicenza).

Invasions by Barbarians in the Middle Ages saw a decline in civilisation, with the Veneti hiding on islands in the coastal lagoons of what would become Venice. In the 6th

Gondola traffic, Venice

century, Justinian conquered Venetia for the Byzantine Eastern Roman Empire, followed by the Lombards whose division of the territory created the Veneto and Friuli regions. Frankish domination followed in the 8th century, while the 9th century saw Berenger of Friuli crowned king of Italy.

## Venice

Venice is Italy's most enchanting and most exotic city – and with good reason. After a short period of Byzantine rule in the 8th century, the city-state became a wealthy independent republic ruled by a doge, becoming one of the most influential empires of the Middle Ages and Renaissance. Successful at maritime trade, Venice dominated the Mediterranean for over 1,000 years,

Veneto and Friuli-Venezia Giulia

A gold mosaic at Basilica di San Marco

A wonderful city to walk through, you can expect dimly lit alleys that snake between splendid palaces, seemingly heading nowhere until they arrive at a pretty arched bridge to be crossed or open onto an expansive square lined with cafés demanding you pull up a chair and relax to savour the scene. Occasionally the alleys lead to a dead end, but that's part of the delight.

While some of the fun of exploring Venice is the ability to get off the beaten track and still get lost in a city that is well signposted, there are some essential sights you should make a beeline for. Keep in mind that Venice is one of the most visited cities in the world and the crowds of tourists can be maddening. It's impossible to avoid them, but there are a few golden rules: never visit Venice during the summer when the ever-diminishing local population takes its vacation and Venice is dominated by tourists; see the

ruling the Veneto and Friuli, as well as Lombardia and Romagna, Istria and Dalmatia (now part of Croatia), Cefalonia, Corfu, Crete, Ithaca and Zante (in Greece), and Cyprus. The Venetians protected their outposts with impressive fortifications and the colonies prospered. It wasn't until 1797, following Napoleon's invasion, that the Republic was dissolved and handed to the Austrian Empire until 1866 when, after the Third War of Independence, it was annexed to Italy.

The *Serenissima* (serene one), as Venice is fondly called, is easily Italy's most beguiling city. Justifiably famous for its beautiful palaces, lovely canals, atmospheric lanes, exquisite art and architecture, and its handsome gondoliers, Venice is a city that charms at every turn.

## 'BRING YOUR OWN BOTTLE'

For a country that appears to have a water fountain on every corner, it's odd that Italy is reported to have the highest consumption of bottled water per capita in the world. In Venice, the Cardinal asked that the city give up its bottled water obsession for the fasting season of Lent, donating the money saved to water projects in other countries. The project took off and now visitors to the often-stifling city have been asked to contribute. Visitors are given an empty bottle and a map of the 122 fountains across the city, in the hope that their consumption of bottled water will be significantly reduced.

most popular sights (those below) early in the morning; do as the locals do and enjoy a leisurely restaurant lunch and siesta in the afternoon; then explore the streets before and after dinner, when the day-trippers have left.

### Basilica di San Marco (Saint Mark's Basilica)

An awe-inspiring symbol of Venetian power and prosperity, the exuberant Saint Mark's Basilica is simply stunning. Venice's number one tourist attraction and one of Italy's most breathtakingly beautiful cathedrals, it's worth the long wait in line. After a fire in 976 destroyed the original church (built in 828 to house Saint Mark the Evangelist's body), reconstruction started on a new church in 1063. Completed in 1094, it elegantly combined Byzantine and Romanesque styles, boasting five bulbous domes and a Greek cross shape. First serving as the *chiesa ducale*, the doge's private chapel, it became Venice's cathedral in 1807.

What makes San Marco so exotic is its blend of East and West. The bronze horse statues above the entrance were stolen from Constantinople (Istanbul) in 1204, while the enormous chandelier is Byzantine. Highlights include magical gold mosaics, exquisite artwork, Cappella Zen (Zen Chapel), Museo di San Marco (Museum), Battistero (Baptistery), Galleria (Gallery), Santuario (Sanctuary) and the glittering Pala d'Oro, a gilded silver screen

A *vaporetto* on the Grand Canal

*Veneto and Friuli-Venezia Giulia*

embellished with almost 2,000 precious gems and over 250 enamelled panels. Dress modestly; if you're wearing shoestring-strap tops, short skirts or shorts you'll be refused entry.
*Piazza San Marco.*
*Tel: (041) 522 52 05/522 56 97.*
*www.basilicasanmarco.it.*
*Open: May–Sept Mon–Sat 9.30am–5pm, Sun 2–3.30pm; Oct–Apr Mon–Sat 9.30am–4pm, Sun 2–3.30pm.*
*Admission charge (Santuario, Galleria and Museo di San Marco), free admission (Basilica).*
*Vaporetto: San Marco or San Zaccaria.*

Veneto and Friuli-Venezia Giulia

Ca' Pesaro houses a modern art gallery

sculpture of Saint John the Baptist, and, in the sacristy, a triptych of Madonna and Child with Saints, dating to 1488, by Bellini. The elaborate tombs belong to two of Venice's greatest artists – the pyramid-shaped tomb is that of sculptor Antonio Canova, while opposite is an imposing memorial to Titian.
*Campo dei Frari, San Polo.*
*Tel: (041) 272 86 18. Open: Mon–Sat 9am–6pm, Sun 1–6pm. Admission charge. Vaporetto: San Tomà.*

### Ca' d'Oro (Golden Palace) and Ca' Sagrado (Sacred Palace)

In the glorious Venetian Gothic style for which Venice is famous, Ca' d'Oro or the Golden Palace was once decorated in pure gold. Given by Venetian patrician Marino Contarini to his wife in 1434, and then by a 19th-century Russian prince to renowned dancer Maria Taglioni, its final owner gave it to the city of Venice, along with exquisite contents that now form the collection of Galleria Franchetti and include ancient antiquities, paintings, sculptures and precious art objects. Next door, the 15th-century Ca' Sagrado is now a luxury hotel.
*Ca' d'Oro, Calle Ca' d'Oro, Cannaregio.*
*Tel: (041) 523 87 90. www.cadoro.org.*
*Open: Tue–Sun 8am–7pm. Closed: Mon.*
*Admission charge. Vaporetto: Ca' d'Oro.*

### Ca' Pesaro

This splendid Baroque palace by Baldassare Longhena was finished in 1710, some thirty years after the

### Basilica di Santa Maria Gloriosa dei Frari (Saint Mary of the Friars)

Considered Venice's next most beautiful church after San Marco, Santa Maria Gloriosa dei Frari was established by Franciscan friars (*frari*) in 1252 after the doge gave them an old abbey in San Polo which they replaced with this colossal Gothic structure. Inside are intricately carved choir stalls, stunning Titian altarpieces, Donatello's wooden

architect died. It's home to the Galleria Internazionale d'Arte Moderna (Gallery of Modern Art), boasting an engaging collection including Kandinsky, Klimt and Matisse, and the Museo d'Arte Orientale (Oriental Art Museum), featuring a fascinating array of art, armour, costumes and musical instruments from the East.
*Santa Croce 2076.*
*Tel: (041) 524 06 95.*
*Open: Tue–Sun 10am–5pm.*
*Closed Mon. Admission charge.*
*Vaporetto: San Stae.*

## Ca' Rezzonico

Another beautiful Baroque palace designed by Longhena, Ca' Rezzonico was once the home of English poet Robert Browning's son. Browning actually died here from a cold. Decorated with marble and frescoes, its salons gilded and filled with plush furnishings, glittering chandeliers, and over 300 works of art, including pieces by Tintoretto and Carriera, it's now home to the Museo del Settecento Veneziano (Museum of 18th-Century Venice), and provides a revealing insight into the everyday life of Venetian nobles.
*Museo del Settecento Veneziano, Fondamenta Rezzonico, Dorsoduro.*
*Tel: (041) 241 01 00.*
*www.galleriacarezzonico.com. Open: Apr–Oct daily 10am–6pm; Nov–Mar daily 10am–5pm. Admission charge.*
*Vaporetto: Ca' Rezzonico.*

## Campanile di San Marco and Piazza San Marco
## (Saint Mark's Campanile and Square)

After visiting the basilica, climb up the 98.6m (323ft) high campanile, the splendid brick bell tower on Piazza San Marco, to marvel at the spectacular vistas of Venice, the Lido, the surrounding region and, on a clear day, the Alps. The campanile has an astonishing history – having survived

Early morning is the best time to visit the Piazza San Marco

Veneto and Friuli-Venezia Giulia

some 1,000 years, in 1902 the mighty tower collapsed suddenly. A new tower, built to the same plan, was completed by 1912. Piazza di San Marco is where tourists spend much of their time – feeding the pigeons and taking photos of each other doing so – and it can get very crowded so it is best visited early in the morning or in the evening when the day-trippers have gone.

A fun thing to do is savour an *aperitivo* while listening to the pianist at **Caffè Florian** (*tel: (041) 520 56 41*). Inaugurated in 1720, it's Venice's oldest café, and Dickens, Proust and Casanova all sipped something here. Sitting inside is less expensive, but it's more entertaining to sit under the arcades and enjoy the action on the square.

Palazzo Ducale, the Doge's Palace

*Campanile, Tel: (041) 522 40 64.*
*Open: Apr–Sept daily 9.30am–5.30pm;*
*Oct–Mar daily 9.30am–4.30pm.*
*Admission charge. Vaporetto: San Marco*
*or San Zaccaria.*

## Chiesa di Santo Stefano (Saint Stephen's Church)

Founded in the 13th century by Augustinian hermits, the convent of Santo Stefano is Venice's third largest. Spookily, the church was rebuilt in the 14th century and consecrated some six times following the recurring appearance of bloodstains on the ceiling. As you enter, note the stunning portal by Bartolomeo Bon and, inside, the impressive pillars in a florid Gothic style. The wooden roof, shaped like a ship's keel, was built by some of the lagoon's master shipbuilders.
*Campo Santo Stefano, San Marco.*
*Tel: (041) 275 04 62. Open: Mon–Sat*
*10am–5pm, Sun 1–5pm.*
*Admission charge. Vaporetto: Accademia,*
*Sant Angelo or San Marco.*

## Gallerie dell'Accademia (Accademia Art Gallery)

Founded by Napoleon in 1807, it houses the world's finest collection of Venetian art, gathered from *scuole* (brotherhoods), churches and convents that Napoleon deemed unworthy of holding such important works. On display are significant examples of Byzantine art and Venetian Gothic (including 14th-century works by Paolo Veneziano), Venetian Renaissance (including vivid paintings and altarpieces by 15th-century master Jacopo Bellini and his son Giovanni, as well as Tintoretto and Veronese). Notable works include those by 16th-century giant Titian, the Venetian Republic's official painter, paintings by Renaissance artists Gentile Bellini and Vittore Carpaccio, frescoes by Giambattista Tiepolo, and serene landscapes by Antonio Canal ('Canaletto'), another official painter of the Republic. Book in advance to avoid the queues, and hire the informative audio guide.

*Campo della Carità, near Ponte dell'Accademia (Accademia Bridge), Dorsoduro. Tel: (041) 522 22 47, 520 03 45. www.gallerieaccademia.org. Open: Tue–Sun 8am–7pm. Closed: Mon. Admission charge. Vaporetto: Accademia.*

Veneto and Friuli-Venezia Giulia

Water taxi at the Rialto Bridge (*see p95*)

### Palazzo Ducale (Doge's Palace)

No building expresses the wealth and power of Venice at its most magnificent than the spectacular pink and white marble Gothic-Renaissance Doge's Palace adjoining the Basilica on Piazzetta San Marco. First constructed in the 12th century, although continually redecorated and remodelled, it was all at once a house of government, governor's residence, parliament and prison. Prepare to be astonished by the Scala dei Giganti (Stairway of the Giants), guarded by colossal statues of Mars and Neptune, the staggeringly lavish Scala d'Oro (Golden Staircase), and the enormous

array of art, including paintings and ceiling frescoes by Tintoretto and Veronese. One of the most popular attractions is the enclosed, marble Ponte dei Sospiri (Bridge of Sighs), above a small canal separating the Palace from the prison. It was named after the sighs heard from prisoners being led along here to execution. A guided tour visits the doge's apartments, the torture chambers and the prison – its most infamous resident was Venetian-born author, libertine and freemason Giacomo Casanova (1725–98). Imprisoned in 1755, he and his accomplice would be the only prisoners ever to escape.

(*Cont. on p.96*)

# Cruise: Venice Grand Canal

*This cruise along the 4km (2½ miles) long Grand Canal is a wonderful introduction to Venice, taking in its main bridges, sights, museums and splendid palaces. Do the cruise in the morning and it will be a bright bustling affair. Around sunset, Venice is at its most mesmerising, but after dark when lights illuminate the palaces and bridges it is at its most romantic.*

*Allow around half an hour for a one-way trip without stops and a whole day with stops.*

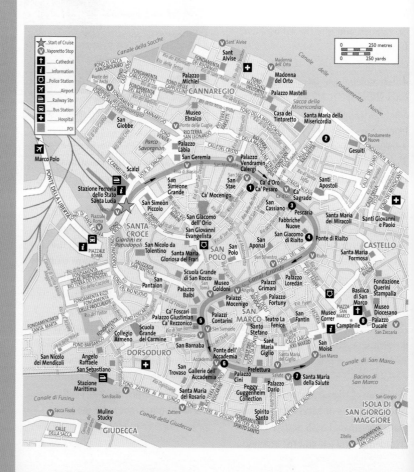

*Start at the Ferrovia vaporetto stop. It stops at Riva di Biasio, then San Marcuola, and then Campo San Stae. Ca' Pesaro is the first palace on the right after departing the wharf.*

*Before boarding, buy a 24-hour or 72-hour card, rather than single tickets, as you will find yourself using the vaporetti constantly. Once on board, secure a seat outside at the front for the best views.*

## 1 Ca' Pesaro
*See pp90–91.*
*At the next vaporetto stop, Ca' d'Oro, three opulent palaces stand on the left.*

## 2 Ca' d'Oro and Ca' Sagrado
*See p90.*
*Diagonally opposite, on the right side of the canal, are two bustling squares.*

## 3 Campo di Pescaria and Campo San Giacomo di Rialto
The waterside Campo di Pescaria (Square of the Fishmongers) is home to Venice's daily fish market and, beside it, the fresh fruit and vegetable market. The adjoining Campo San Giacomo di Rialto is home to some excellent *enoteche.*
*Go back to the vaporetto. It takes you to Venice's most famous bridge.*

## 4 Ponte di Rialto (Rialto Bridge)
Venice's oldest bridge, a pontoon bridge when established in 1181, was replaced by a wooden structure in 1255. That was partially burnt down in 1310, before collapsing from the weight of a crowd enjoying a boat procession in

1524. The current stone bridge was finished in 1591. The two rows of shops in it sell jewellery, leather and glass.
*This stretch of the canal is especially enchanting. There are a number of magnificent palaces including Palazzo Balbi on your right after the San Tomà stop, then Ca' Foscari, Palazzo Giustinian and Ca'Rezzonico.*

## 5 Ca' Rezzonico
*See p91.*
*After Ca' Rezzonico, the next stop is Ponte dell'Accademia, the place to alight for Gallerie di Accademia (see pp92–3).*

## 6 Ponte dell'Accademia
An impressive steel bridge designed by Neville, it was built in 1854, only to be replaced in the 1930s by a wooden structure. Not lasting well, the bridge was deemed unsafe and replaced by another steel bridge in 1985.
*For many, the approach to the splendid Santa Maria della Salute church, on your right, is the highlight of the cruise.*

## 7 Santa Maria della Salute (Church of Saint Mary of Salvation)
Constructed in 1631 to celebrate the end of the plague, this church (*currently closed for renovation*) sits at the entrance to the canal. Designed by Longhena, it has an impressive dome and great art by Titian and Tintoretto.
*Alight at the next stop, San Marco.*

## 8 Piazza San Marco
*See p91.*

*Piazzetta San Marco. Tel: (041) 520 90 70.
Open: Apr–Oct daily 9am–7pm,
Nov–Mar daily 9am–5pm.
Admission charge. Vaporetto: San Marco
or San Zaccaria.*

## Peggy Guggenheim Collection

Married to surrealist artist Max Ernst,
heiress and art collector Peggy
Guggenheim (1898–1979) was the niece
of Solomon Guggenheim, founder of
New York's Guggenheim Museum. Her
home of 30 years, the elegant Palazzo
Venier dei Leoni is a museum housing
her outstanding art collection. Covering
most of the 20th-century art
movements, the exhibition spans
Cubism, Futurism, Abstract art and
Surrealism, and includes works by
Picasso, Braque, Kandinsky, Magritte,
Ernst, Miró, Rothko, Motherwell,
Pollock and Bacon, and, in the lovely
gardens, sculptures by Giacometti.
*Calle San Cristoforo, Dorsoduro.
Tel: (041) 240 54 11. www.guggenheim-
venice.it. Open: Wed–Mon 10am–6pm.
Closed: Tue. Admission charge.
Vaporetto: Accademia or Salute.*

## Scuola Grande di San Rocco
## (Brotherhood of Saint Roch)

Situated in one of the most ornate
buildings in Venice and a fine example
of Venetian Renaissance architecture,

Ornate painted ceiling at Scuola Grande di San Rocco

the Brotherhood of San Rocco is dedicated to one of Venice's patron saints, San Rocco, a medical student who, while caring for plague sufferers, was infected but miraculously healed. Considered as splendid as the Sistine Chapel by many, the building is decorated with a series of some 60 paintings by Tintoretto, painted between 1576 and 1588.

*Campo di San Rocco, San Polo.*
*Tel: (041) 523 48 64.*
*www.scuolagrandesanrocco.it.*
*Open: daily Apr–Oct 9am–5pm;*
*Nov–Mar 10am–5pm. Admission charge.*

**Teatro La Fenice (the Phoenix Theatre)**
Tucked away in the backstreets between Piazza San Marco and Campo San Stefano, La Fenice is one of Italy's oldest and most lavish opera theatres.

The beautifully restored Teatro La Fenice

### VENICE: SINK OR SWIM

The paradox for Venice is that the gorgeous canals that draw millions of people each year hold the same thing that could see those tourists disappear – water. It was way back in November 1966, when a 2m (7ft) flood took out essential services, that people questioned Venice's long-term survival. Studies, arguments, counter-arguments and countless floods passed before Prime Minister Berlusconi inaugurated the MOSE project in 2003. The 78 massive gates, 28m (92ft) wide and 18m (59ft) long, will protect the three inlets to Venice's lake when completed in 2011. Arguments still rage about environmental and economic concerns with the project, but with the city sinking 23cm (9in) in the last 100 years, everyone agrees that something had to be done to save one of the world's great cities.

It's been the venue for some of opera's most unforgettable openings, including Verdi's 1853 premiere of *La Traviata*, which was a dreadful flop. La Fenice was set on fire in 1996 by workers renovating the opera house in an attempt to cover up the fact that their work was incredibly delayed. Virtually rebuilt and restored to its former glory, it opened again in 2004.

*Campo San Fantin, San Marco.*
*Tel: (041) 786 511.*
*www.teatrolafenice.it. Open: daily*
*8am–8pm, performances from 8pm*
*onwards. Audio guide available.*
*Vaporetto: San Marco.*

The castle on Piazza Garibaldi, Asolo

## Asolo

The lovely hilltop village of Asolo is fondly referred to as 'The City of a Hundred Horizons' because of its enchanting vistas of the surrounding mountains from almost any spot within the town. With its elegant old palaces, pretty architecture and atmospheric cobblestone lanes, the charming village is an absolute delight to explore and a wonderful place to spend a few days relaxing or hiking in the nearby hills.

Dating to pre-Roman times, Asolo was an early settlement of the Veneti, and it has a long and fascinating history that, combined with its natural beauty, has attracted equally interesting characters, including the adventurer and travel writer Freya Stark, English poet Robert Browning and actress Eleonora Duse, who all owned houses here. Probably one of the most compelling residents was the former Queen of Cyprus, Caterina Cornaro, who lived in exile here from 1489 after Venice conquered the Cypriot kingdom. Under her patronage, the great artist Gentile Bellini developed as a member of her Asolo court.

There are a few sights worth seeing, including the lovely **Piazza Garibaldi** with its fine fountain and elegant architecture including the Caterina Cornaro's castle (now the Eleonora Duse theatre), the 18th-century **Palazzo della Ragione**'s marvellous loggia and City Museum, and, adjoining it, the splendid **Duomo**, also dating to 1747, with a fine painting by Lorenzo Lotto. Also check out the remains of an ancient amphitheatre in the grounds of Villa Freya. Fans of Freya Stark won't want to miss her grave at the town cemetery, which is also where Eleonora Duse lies.

## Padova

Apart from its basilica and churches, palaces and villas, this lively little city holds few attractions for tourists, yet it's nevertheless a lovely, low-key place to spend a few days relaxing. An important university town, it was home to Dante, Petrarch and Galileo, and its university grounds are wonderful to explore, on foot or by bike.

## Cappella degli Scrovegni (Scrovegni Chapel)

Padova's number one attraction is the Cappella degli Scrovegni, a touchstone for *Rinascimento* (Renaissance) art in Northern Italy. The break away from the Byzantine style to the Proto-Renaissance period (1290–1400) is commonly attributed to the paintings of Giotto di Bondone (*c.*1267–1337). The chapel contains the best known of his works, and the frescoes, focusing on the Virgin Mary's life, were completed around 1305. The work is outstanding because of the emotion depicted in the subjects' faces and the three-dimensionality of the work. Due to deterioration, the Cappella was essentially sealed off in 2000 and now has its own 'microclimate'. Since only 25 people are allowed per visit, booking ahead is essential.

*Chiesa dei Eremitani, Corso Garibaldi. Tel: (049) 201 00 20. www.cappelladegliscrovegni.it. Open: daily 9am–7pm. Admission charge.*

## Treviso

Fondly referred to as 'Little Venice', this small, sophisticated Veneto city features tranquil canals, charming medieval arcades, and beautifully frescoed buildings. Home to successful companies such as the fashion brand Benetton and the sleek home appliance manufacturer DeLonghi, Treviso is an affluent city, and its wealth is evident in the elegant city streets, the well-dressed locals and the excellent shopping.

This is a fabulous town for strolling and whiling away a few hours in a chic bar or café or simply taking in the atmosphere of the lovely squares: Piazza Rinaldi, notable for its three

Chiesa dei Eremitani houses the Cappella degli Scrovegni

Veneto and Friuli-Venezia Giulia

palaces built by the Rinaldi family dating to the 12th, 15th and 18th centuries, Piazza dei Signori and the Palazzo di Podestà, and the lovely Loggia dei Cavalieri, which is Romanesque with Byzantine influences, unlike loggias in other cities in the region which are typically in the Venetian-Gothic styles.

There are also several churches worth seeking out. The impressive *duomo* has seven splendid domes and features works by Titian. The original church dated to late Roman times; however, two chapels and a crypt were added in 1520, and only the original gate is now left from the original building.

The Late Romanesque-Early Gothic **Chiesa di San Francesco** (Saint Francis Church), built by the Franciscan monks between 1231 and 1270, features fine frescoes in its peaceful chapels and the tomb of Pietro Alighieri, son of the poet Dante. Sadly, Napoleon's troops used the church as a stable; however, it was reopened in 1928 after renovation. There are also significant frescoes by Tommaso da Modena in the 13th-century Venetian-Romanesque and French-Gothic **Chiesa di San Nicolò** (Saint Nicholas Church).

Treviso also boasts pretty stone bridges across its canals, of which **Ponte di Pria** (Stone Bridge) is one to look out for at the confluence of the city's Canal Grande and Buranelli canal.

### Trieste

Boasting monumental palaces, vast squares, pretty canals, and atmospheric

Piazza dei Signori in Treviso

Grand buildings surround Trieste's Piazza dell'Unità d'Italia

*belle époque* Vienna-style coffee houses, Trieste is one of Northern Italy's most elegant cities. Highly underrated and often overlooked by travellers, it may not be big on tourist attractions but it makes a wonderful place to relax for a couple of days – this is a city where time should be spent exploring the tiny old town, relaxing for a few hours in a café, and strolling along the waterfront.

Trieste has a unique culture and a Slavic feel, due partly to its proximity to Slovenia and Croatia, and its history as part of the independent 'Free Territory of Trieste'. This territory included the Croatian region of Istria, and wasn't divided until 1975, when Trieste was given to Italy. Trieste also has a large population of Central and Eastern European immigrants and tourists who come here to shop.

Once the main port of the Austro-Hungarian empire, in recent years the city has cleaned up its waterfront and opened it up to create wide seaside promenades overlooking the sparkling Adriatic Sea. This is a lovely place to take a walk in the late afternoon or early evening and there are several ice-cream trucks on the waterfront to make it even more inviting.

Trieste's café culture rivals Vienna's, with grand, ornate cafés decorated with mirrors on the walls, elaborate chandeliers, enormous picture windows, and terraces out front where the locals love to sit in the sun reading a newspaper and sipping the city's superb coffee.

A race through the hilly streets of Udine

The most famous cafés are the mirror-filled **Caffè Degli Specchi** (*Piazza dell'Unità d'Italia 7*); the Art Deco **Antico Caffè San Marco** (*Via Battisti 18*), once a meeting place for the city's intellectuals; and local favourite, **Caffè Tommaseo** (*Piazza Tommaseo 4*), dating to 1830, where there's occasionally live jazz in the evenings. Kick-start your exploration with a coffee at Caffè Degli Specchi from where you can take in the splendid architecture of the grand sprawling Piazza dell'Unità d'Italia, where concerts are held in the summertime. Stand in the middle of the square and look around – you're surrounded by majestic palaces, including the **Palazzo Communale** (Town Hall), on three sides, and on the fourth the sea.

## Udine

This elegant town in the hills north of Trieste, tucked between the Adriatic and the Alps, is only 40km (25 miles) from Slovenia, so, like Trieste, it has a decidedly Slavic and Central European feel about it. It's a wonderful place to spend a day or two. There's an attractive main square, outstanding Tiepolo frescoes and, like Trieste, a lively café society, as well as restaurants serving delicious food with an Eastern European flavour.

Start exploring at the main square, **Piazza della Libertà**, where there are two enchanting Venetian-Gothic style *loggias*. The first, at the town hall, is **Loggia del Lionello**, dating to 1448, while opposite is the Renaissance-style **Loggia di San Giovanni**. Note the imposing clock tower, **Torre dell'Orologio**, modelled on the tower on Piazza San Marco in Venice. It also dates to 1448; however, it was damaged by fire in 1876 and rebuilt to a new design. Also on the square is the elegant fountain by Bergamo architect Giovanni Carrara, built in 1542, and splendid columns topped with the ubiquitous Venetian Lion and statues dedicated to Hercules and Cacus, and Justice and Peace. A short hike up the hill from here is Udine's Venetian Castle, built in 1517 on top of the ruins of a Lombard fortress.

Don't miss **Chiesa di Santa Maria della Purità** for fine 18th-century frescoes by Giambattista Tiepolo and his son Domenico, and the imposing

**Duomo**, dating to 1236, although it was altered considerably in the 18th century. The cathedral also boasts paintings by Tiepolo, as well as noted artists Amalteo and Dorigny. It features a beautiful Baroque interior and a lavish chapel decorated with frescoes by Vitale da Bologna dating to 1349.

## Verona

A popular leisure destination since Julius Caesar used to holiday here, and written about by great literary travellers Goethe and Stendhal, Verona is the Veneto's most visited city after Venice. It's also one of the region's most romantic cities, partly because of its beautifully preserved medieval and Renaissance architecture and atmospheric cobblestone streets, but mostly due to it being the setting for William Shakespeare's play *Romeo and Juliet*. While the actual existence of a real-life Romeo and Juliet is doubtful, a balcony at Villa Capuleti is one of Verona's most popular attractions.

Verona flourished for a number of centuries, at its peak politically and culturally during the 13th and 14th centuries under the ruthless Scaligeri (or della Scala) dynasty (you'll notice their heraldic emblem, the *scala*, a ladder, as you explore Verona), and then again under Venetian rule when it became a regional capital.

Veneto and Friuli-Venezia Giulia

The Scaligeri family tombs in Verona

### Arena di Verona (Verona Arena)

For almost 2,000 years this amphitheatre has held everything from gladiatorial exhibitions to concerts by rock band REM. Arguably the world's best-preserved Roman amphitheatre, it's indisputably the third-biggest remaining Roman theatre worldwide, having, in its initial guise, held 30,000 people. Built in AD 30, its original pink-and-white limestone façade was almost completely destroyed in the earthquake of 1117, with sections of it carted off for other building projects, a common occurrence at the time. Restoration efforts began during the Renaissance, and since 1913 it has been the site for one of the most famous opera seasons during summer, when the balmy air

### YE OLDE VERONA

The affection for William Shakespeare's 1597 play, *Romeo and Juliet*, is no more apparent than on the streets of fair Verona. But it's not an original Shakespeare saga. The tale of the 'star-cross'd lovers' is based on a story by Luigi da Porto, who wrote the narrative in Vicenza in 1530. The two families at the centre of the book, Montecchi and Capuleti, did exist in Verona, becoming the Montagues and Capulets in Shakespeare's play. As the characters themselves were fictional, all of the tourism marketing around *Romeo and Juliet* is as fictional as the story itself – but all power to 'The Bard' for writing such a compelling play that still captures people's imaginations!

heightens the wonderful acoustics of the theatre.

*Piazza Brà. Tel: (045) 800 32 04. www.arena.it. Open: Sept–Jun Mon 2–7.30pm, Tue–Sun 8.30am–7pm; Jul–Aug (summer opera season) daily 9am–3.30pm. Admission charge.*

### Castelvecchio

Long the home and headquarters of Verona's noble rulers, this imposing fortress now hosts the **Museo di Castelvecchio**, the city's museum, and holds a superb collection of weapons, paintings, sculptures, costumes, jewellery and other precious objects of historical interest.

*Corso Castelvecchio. Tel: (045) 806 26 11. Open: Tue–Sun 8.30am–7.30pm. Closed: Mon. Admission charge.*

### Duomo

Unlike most Italian cities, Verona's cathedral isn't situated on the main

The summer opera season at the Arena di Verona

Ponte Scaligero and the Castelvecchio, Verona

square, but rather on the small Piazza del Duomo. It features a fascinating combination of architectural styles but is mostly Romanesque, with intricately detailed carvings on the enormous doors.
*Piazza del Duomo. Tel: (045) 592 813. Open: Mar–Oct Mon–Sat 9.30am–6pm, Sun 1–6pm; Nov–Feb Mon–Sat 10am–4pm, Sun 1.30–4pm. Admission charge.*

### Vicenza

With historic ties to Venice, and once known as the 'Mainland Venice', Vicenza's canals were once linked to those of Venice. The small but elegant city is most notable, however, for its classical architecture by Palladio, which has earned the city and surrounding region a place on the UNESCO Heritage Site listing as 'City of Vincenza and the Palladian Villas of

the Veneto'. The city is home to 23 graceful buildings by Palladio, including the Teatro Olimpico (Olympic Theatre), Basilica Palladiana, Palazzo Chiericati (Vicenza's city museum), Palazzo Barbaran Da Porto, Palazzo Thiene and Villa Capra, known as 'La Rotonda'.

Like many of Northern Italy's cities and towns, Vicenza boasts beautiful churches, many of them filled with art, including the 13th-century Chiesa di Ara Coeli, featuring works by Tiepolo and the 11th-century Duomo, restored in the 16th and 19th centuries. The **Pinacoteca Civica** (Municipality Art Gallery. *Palazzo Chiericati, Piazza Matteotti 37/39. Tel: (0444) 222 811. www.museicivicivicenza.it. Open: Tue–Sun 9–7pm. Closed: Mon. Admission charge*) also features fine paintings by local artists.

# Walk: Verona

*This relaxed ramble around old Verona takes in this romantic city's main attractions, including atmospheric Roman sites such as the massive Arena, the imposing fortress Castelvecchio, marvellous squares boasting beautiful frescoed edifices, several stately churches, and spectacular city vistas from several locations.*

*Allow 2½ hours for the walk, although this could be extended to 8 hours including church and museum visits.*

*Start on the main square, semi-circular café-lined Piazza Brà.*

## 1  Piazza Brà

Arriving from the old town you enter through Portoni della Brà (Brà's 'little door'), from where Palazzo della Gran Guardia is to the left, Teatro Filarmonico is also left, and back to the right is Palazzo Barbieri. Directly ahead is the Roman arena, dominating the square.

*Follow Via Roma to Corso Castelvecchio.*

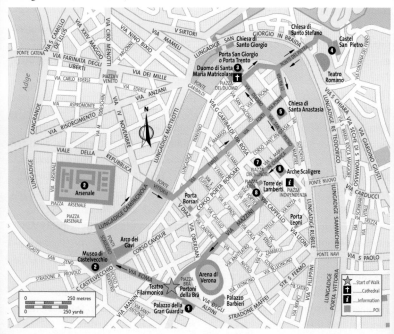

## 2 Castelvecchio (Old Castle) and Arsenale

The enormous red brick Castelvecchio is an impressive crenellated fortress with colossal walls and towers. Amble under the arches and cross Ponte Scaligero (Scaligero Bridge) to admire the stately Arsenal before sauntering along Lungadige Campagnola.

*Cross Ponte Vittoria to Via Armando Diaz. Turn left onto Via San Michele alla Porta, which becomes Via Francesco Emilei then Via Forti. Turn left on Via Duomo.*

## 3 Duomo

Admire the ornate exterior of Verona's mainly Romanesque Duomo (*see pp104–5*).

*Go over Ponte del Pietra, cross Regaste Redentore, then follow the stairs and path snaking up to Castel San Pietro.*

## 4 Castel San Pietro

From the gardens there are panoramic views over old Verona. To the right is Chiesa di Santo Stefano, then, beyond this, Chiesa di Santo Giorgio. Directly ahead is the Duomo (right of the bridge) and Chiesa di Santa Anastasia (to the left). Beyond is Torri dei Lamberti.

*Return via the path. Cross the bridge again. Turn left onto Via Ponte di Pietra, then follow it round to the church.*

## 5 Chiesa di Santa Anastasia

This brick Gothic church, although never finished, is nevertheless impressive. It boasts a 15th-century

gate, a Gothic portal dating to 1330, and inside, vivid frescoes.

*Turn left onto Via San Pietro and right into Santa Maria in Chiavica.*

## 6 Arche Scaligere

The Arche Scaligere (Scaligeri Tombs) are the Gothic marble tombs of the Scaligeri family. The most attention-grabbing is that above the dynasty's chapel of Cangrande I ('Big Dog') sitting atop his horse, with his *cani* (dogs) by his side.

*Corner of Via delle Arche Scaligeri and Via della Costa. No entry to the courtyard itself.*

*Continue to Piazza dei Signori.*

## 7 Piazza dei Signori

This elegant square has at its centre a statue of Dante, who, exiled from Florence, was the guest of Cangrande I. The crenellated edifice is the 13th-century Scaligeri home, the building behind Dante is 15th-century Loggia del Consiglio (Portico of the Counsel), while facing Dante is Romanesque **Palazzo della Ragione**.

*Between Via Mazzini and Corso Porta Borsari. Palazzo: Tel: (049) 820 5006. Open: Mon–Sat 8am–7pm. Admission charge. Continue to Piazza Erbe.*

## 8 Piazza Erbe

While the market stalls on lively 'Square of the Herbs' selling fresh produce and flowers can be distracting, step back to take in the splendid buildings.

*Stroll along Via Giuseppe Mazzini to return to Piazza Brà.*

# Trentino-Alto Adige

*Boasting the most breathtaking mountain scenery in Italy (if not Europe) in the Dolomites, a wealth of wonderful outdoors activities, splendid Alpine towns such as Cortina d'Ampezzo, and some of the most delightful Austro-German cities in Bolzano and Merano, Trentino-Alto Adige is arguably one of Northern Italy's most alluring and engaging regions.*

Trentino-Alto Adige, or Trentino-Südtirol in German, is an autonomous region consisting of two provinces, Trento and Bolzano (Bozen), and has a long and fascinating history, dating back to the conquest of the region by the Romans in 15 BC, when some of the towns were used as garrisons to protect northern trade routes. It would later be split between the Bavarians, Lombards and Alamanni, and after Charlemagne created the Kingdom of Italy, Trento would form the frontier. Governed by prince-bishops from Trento and Brixen from the 11th century, it was given to the Austrian Habsburg family in 1363, being Germanised during this period. The area later formed part of the Austro-Hungarian Empire (from 1815) until it was returned to Italy once again in 1919.

Bordered by the Austrian Tyrol in the north, Switzerland (Graubünden) to the northwest, Lombardy in the west and Veneto in the south, the region is staggeringly beautiful. Lush green meadows are dotted with wildflowers in the spring and summer, and blanketed by snow in winter. The rugged limestone Dolomites rise dramatically from these emerald fields and tower into the heavens, their summits in the clouds.

While the region is a hugely popular winter destination for skiers and snowboarders (and also for those just looking to curl up with a good book in front of a fireplace somewhere), especially the resorts of Madonna di Campiglio and Cortina d'Ampezzo, it is almost as popular in summer with walkers.

Hiking trails crisscross the ranges, with routes offering something for all levels of walkers from the tourist out for a stroll to the experienced mountaineer looking for a challenge. On the mountain plateaux, wooden log cabins reside beside still lakes, providing refuge to trekkers, climbers and cross-country skiers.

In the valley basins pretty Alpine villages of Swiss-style wooden chalets with window boxes of geraniums spill down the slopes. Vineyards sprawl across the hills on lower ground, their grapevines growing on steep terraces, on riverbanks, in every inconceivable space imaginable – just like everywhere else in Italy.

Wine is an important industry here, as it is everywhere in Northern Italy, although the locals are just as likely to be downing a German beer as they might a light aromatic glass of white. As expected from a region that is cold for far longer than it is hot, the cuisine is rustic, heavy and hearty, partly influenced by the Austro-German heritage.

The cities and towns of the north, such as Bolzano, Bressanone and Merano, also reflect that Austro-German heritage, in their architecture, culture and language – you're more likely to hear German spoken in these parts. But then there's Cortina, which is as chic and sophisticated as Italian cities come.

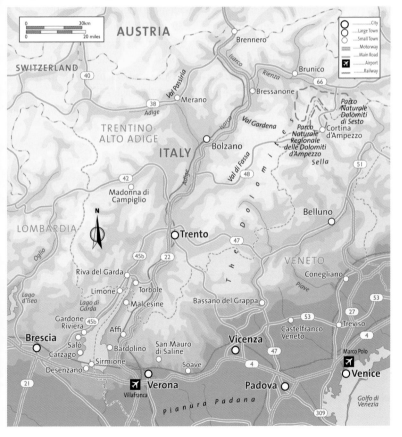

## Trento

Trento must have one of the most strikingly beautiful town squares of any Italian city in its Piazza del Duomo, with its frescoed buildings, colossal Romanesque Duomo, crenellated fortress, and splendid Fontana del Nettuno (Neptune's Fountain) at its centre.

The main square really comes alive on a sunny day when its cafés are filled with locals and tourists alike, all eating elaborate *gelato* desserts. A lively university city, Trento has more of a youthful vibe than other cities in the region, with an engaging programme of art, culture and music held throughout the year at various locations around the city. It also has one of the best tourism offices in the region with stacks of information, excellent itinerary suggestions, guided tours, and the great-value Trento Card that gives free admission to all of the main attractions.

### Castello del Buonconsiglio (Buonconsiglio Castle)

On the edge of the Old Town (across the road from a car park which is handy for all the sights, if you're driving) and set in leafy grounds is the imposing 'Castle of Good Counsel', the fortress of Trento's prince-bishops. It's a mishmash of architectural styles, combining austere 13th-century medieval fortifications with more elaborate Renaissance features. The highlight is the endearing 15th-century frescoes depicting the *ciclo dei mesi* (cycle of the months) from everyday medieval life, in the *Torre dell'Aquila* (Eagle's Tower).
*Via Bernardo Clesio 5. Tel: (0461) 23 37 70. www.buonconsiglio.it.*
*Open: Tue–Sun 10am–6pm.*
*Closed: Mon. Admission charge.*

The cathedral and fortress on Piazza del Duomo

Castello del Buonconsiglio

## Chiesa di Santa Maria Maggiore (Church of Saint Mary)

Although it can't compete in size, this Renaissance church is much more beautiful than the cathedral with its elaborate ceiling decorated with frescoes and stucco, and its pretty rose window that lets in just enough light to create a moody atmosphere. The church was the location of sessions during the Council of Trent (*see box*).
*Vicolo Orsoline 1. Tel: (0461) 23 00 37. Open: daily 8.30am–noon & 2.30–6pm. Free admission.*

## Duomo (Cathedral of San Virgilio)

The immense cathedral, on Trento's equally enormous main square, features a pretty decorated portal, a frescoed ceiling, said to be a copy of Bernini's at Saint Peter's in Rome, and a rather sombre crucifix. It's rather austere and is impressive mostly for its sheer size.
*Piazza del Duomo. Tel: (0461) 98 01 32. Open: daily 9am–noon & 2.30–8pm. Free admission.*

## Palazzo Pretorio (Pretorio Palace)

Adjoining the cathedral, this 13th-century fortress with its square crenellations was home to the bishop-princes until they moved to more secure digs up the road at the Castello del Buonconsiglio. The massive palazzo now houses the Museo Diocesano Tridentino, and even if you're not a fan of religious relics, you'll appreciate the fine 16th-century tapestries, beautifully carved wooden statues and altars, and paintings depicting the Council of Trent (*see box*).
*Piazza del Duomo 18.*
*Tel: (0461) 23 44 19. Open: Wed–Mon 9.30am–12.30pm & 2–5.30pm. Closed: Tue. Admission charge.*

### THE COUNCIL OF TRENT

One of the pivotal historical events in Trento was the 19th ecumenical council of the Roman Catholic Church, more popularly known as the Council of Trent (1545–63). Meeting in 25 sessions held between bouts of internal fighting and extended interruptions, this council was the official response to the questions raised by the Protestant Reformation. The result was a strengthened Roman Catholic Church that regained much of its lost credibility in Europe and is the basis of the Catholic Church today.

The Duomo from Piazza Walther

## Bolzano

Bolzano is a buzzy, sophisticated city. The capital of the autonomous Alto Adige province, it possesses a distinctly Austrian-Germanic flavour that can be disarming to visitors who have been travelling around Italy for a while and have become accustomed to the Italian language, culture and cuisine. But that's what also makes it so refreshing and so much fun.

The stalls at the city's wonderful street food market on Piazza delle Erbe display delicious treats that you're more likely to eat in an Austrian or German town than an Italian one, such as sausages and sauerkraut on a bread roll, washed down with a beer. After work, Bolzano is more Italian, especially in the summer, when *aperitivo* hour is as popular here as it is in Milan and the stylish cafés on Piazza Walther really hum.

## Duomo (Cathedral)

The elegant spire and tiled roof really set Bolzano's splendid 12th-century Gothic cathedral apart from others in the region. While it's easy to be content with gazing at the lovely exterior, there are some fine frescoes inside dating to the 14th and 15th centuries. Also look for the decorative grape-harvest scenes on the Porta del Vino (wine gate) which signify the importance of wine-growing to the region.
*Piazza Walther. Tel: (0471) 97 86 76. Open: daily 10am–noon & 2–5pm. Free admission.*

## Museion (Museum of Modern and Contemporary Art)

This new, cutting-edge contemporary art museum is an 'open' museum, in

### THE ICEMAN COMETH

Over 5,000 years ago, a man wearing goatskin leggings, a grass cape, leather snow boots, and carrying climbing and hunting gear, including an axe, bow and arrow, and other equipment, died on the icy Schnalstal glacier. It wasn't until 1991 that he was accidentally found just inside the border with Austria. It was the greatest find of a mummified body in Europe and an instant archaeological sensation. Because of the state of preservation, Ötzi, as he became known, offered great insight to archaeologists studying Chalcolithic (Copper Age) Europeans. But as scientific analysis improves, Ötzi may reveal more about life during this time – so Ötzi is back 'on ice' at the South Tyrol Museum of Archaeology.

both the sense of the physical design of the display space and the fact that exhibitions are shown in a number of different public locations. Exhibitions promise to be innovative, audacious and relevant if the first shows are anything to go by, such as the exhibition 'Sonic Youth etc: Sensational Fix', which explored the movement of filmmakers, artists and writers working with the band in the 1980s as well as the band's own multimedia work.

*Via Dante 6. Tel: (0471) 22 34 11. www.museion.it. Open: Tue–Sun 10am–8pm, Thur 2–10pm. Closed: Mon. Admission charge.*

## Museo Archeologico dell'Alto Adige (South Tyrol Archaeological Museum)

Although this museum makes compelling use of models, dioramas, stereoscopic pictures, video and multimedia to document the history of the region from the Palaeolithic and Mesolithic Age (15,000 BC) to the Carolingian period (around AD 800), most people are here to see Ötzi, Europe's oldest mummified body (*see box opposite*).

*Via Museo 43. Tel: (0471) 32 01 00. www.iceman.it. Open: Tue–Sun 10am–5.30pm. Closed: Mon. Admission charge.*

Trentino-Alto Adige

Bolzano's Piazza Walther is a hive of activity after dark

# The mighty Dolomites

The mighty Dolomites are one of the most striking sets of mountain ranges in the world. They also provide Italians with a brilliant playground in both summer and winter. The region boasts 18 separate peaks busting the clouds at over 3,000m (9,850ft). The characteristic rocks of the region, dolomitic limestone, have been eroded to form impressive and often fascinating shapes that sometimes appear as if they've been carved by a chisel.

The picturesque Sella mountains

The Dolomites stretch toward Switzerland to the west of the region, and Austria in the north and east. At their centre is the city of Bolzano, a fascinating destination in its own right, but also a great base from which to explore the region. Which part to explore depends on what kind of activities you want to undertake and what time of the year it is.

Summer and winter are equally popular, less so autumn and spring. Summer is dedicated to hiking, climbing and biking, while winter sees all forms of winter sports undertaken, from World Cup ski races to bobsled. If you're hoping for a white Christmas, be warned that Santa can be a bit unreliable in dropping snow on the villages, but the upper ski areas will generally be fine for skiers and snowboarders. Good cover lasts until April, with February the most snow-sure time.

For hikers, June through to September is the best time for trekking, when the trails are far less prone to ice. If you're on a driving trip around the region, note that many small village shops and hotels are shut in the off-seasons and that during the height of winter some roads high in the Alps may be

The views from the road are spectacular

frequently closed – or just *very* slow due to snowfalls.

The best and most rewarding drive (and driving is by far the most convenient way to see the region) is along the Grande Strada delle Dolomiti, the Great Dolomites Road (*see p118*). Right at the heart of the region, the Sella mountain range offers superb vistas and a trip from Cortina d'Ampezzo to Bolzano passes through the Val di Fassa and Val Gardena, with breathtaking scenery.

Hiking in summer is very popular in the region and you'll find places like Cortina d'Ampezzo and Madonna di Campiglio just as busy in July as January! Trails cater to all levels of fitness and bravery: 'T' (tourist), 'H' (hiking), 'EE' (expert hikers) and 'EEA'

(equipped expert hikers). Cortina and Madonna are the best bases from which to do hikes and also organise climbs, as there are mountain-climbing schools and guides available in both towns. Both resorts also have mountain-bike trails and ski lifts run to transport riders for the run of a lifetime.

Both Cortina d'Ampezzo and Madonna di Campiglio are the centres for winter sports in the region. Cortina has the history, a magnificent setting and great beginners' areas, but for those skiers and snowboarders who don't even stop for lunch, the better lift system of Madonna di Campiglio will be a deciding factor. The snowpark and party-town atmosphere attracts a younger, less 'fur coat' crowd as well.

## Bressanone

Bressanone (Brixen in German) shares a common history and culture with Merano. Once a Roman garrison city, it was also ruled by the Austrian Empire until handed to Italy after World War I. Its inhabitants speak German and Italian. Beautifully set in a lush valley at the confluence of two rivers, the Isarco and Rienz, Bressanone has a few engaging sights; however, it's a lot bigger than Merano and doesn't have as much charm.

The Baroque **Duomo**, founded in the 10th century, although rebuilt in the 13th and 18th centuries, features an impressive ceiling fresco, while the 13th-century Renaissance Palazzo dei Principi Vescovi (Bishop's Palace) is elegant. There's also a quaint **Pharmaziemuseum Brixen** (Pharmacy Museum. *Via Ponte Aquila 4. Tel: (0472) 209 112. www.pharmazie.it. Open: Sept–Jun Tue–Wed 2–6pm, Sat 11am–4pm; Jul & Aug Mon–Fri 2–6pm, Sat 11am–4pm. Admission charge),* atmospherically set in a 500-year-old building, charting the development of the town's pharmacy as it traces the history of the profession.

## Cortina d'Ampezzo

Stunningly situated in an emerald valley – snow-white in winter of course – and surrounded by the Dolomites, this fashionable Italian mountain resort has been attracting affluent Europeans to its elegant cobblestone streets and mountain slopes for more than a century. Cortina first grabbed the world's attention when the Winter Olympics were held here in 1956, and it's continued to attract celebrities and royalty ever since.

With its imposing church and grand old hotels in the main pedestrian area, and wooden chalets around town, the

Shopping in Corso Italia, Cortina d'Ampezzo

setting is postcard-perfect, especially in the lead-up to Christmas when the main square hosts a colossal illuminated Christmas tree.

While the younger snowboarding set head to Madonna di Campiglio, Cortina remains a favourite with a more mature, moneyed crowd, which explains the antique stores, art galleries and fur shops lining the main street. Much more Italian in feel than its Germanic neighbours, Cortina's refined cuisine, swish shopping, walking trails and sunny cafés make it more compelling than other Dolomite towns and mean it's a winter destination that can be enjoyed by non-skiers.

Having said that, there are some 450 chairlifts and gondolas to swoosh you up to 1,200km (745 miles) of runs, making Cortina a fantastic base for skiing and snowboarding, as well as hiking, trekking and climbing. The local tourist office can provide information and lists of guides from the mountaineering, skiing and snowboarding schools. For the brave, there's also the opportunity to have a go at hurtling down an Olympic bobsled course, with professionals of course.

Cortina d'Ampezzo's Duomo

## Merano

Splendidly situated in the Val Passiria (Passeier Valley) and surrounded by majestic mountains up to 3,335m (10,950ft) high, Merano is a town of cobblestone streets and *gelato*-coloured buildings with graceful arcades. It's also a popular spa town, beloved by Germans and Italians for its thermal waters.

Merano's fascinating history dates back to its 15 BC founding by the Romans as a garrison called Castrum Majense. Part of the Ostrogothic kingdom in the 5th and 6th centuries, it was ruled by the Habsburgs from 1363. When Napoleon defeated the Austrians, Merano went to the Kingdom of Bavaria, not returning to Italy until World War I when it was determined there were more Italian speakers than German ones within its boundaries. These days, German seems to be spoken more than Italian.

While Merano is a popular winter skiing destination, it's loveliest in the summer when its hills are alive with hikers, summer concerts are held, and the evening *passeggiatta* sees Italians and Germans promenading along its enchanting streets.

# Drive: The Dolomites

*This rewarding drive passes through some of Italy's most staggeringly beautiful scenery as it takes you through the heart of the Dolomites along the Grande Strada delle Dolomiti, or Great Dolomites Road (the SS48). The dramatic route meanders through pretty Alpine villages set against magnificent mountains topped by jagged limestone peaks.*

*Allow 1 full day, with stops for exploring and lunch.*

*You could consider stretching this drive to cover 3–7 days and spend time hiking, skiing or relaxing at spas.*

## 1 Bolzano

Enjoy this vibrant mountain city (*see pp112–13*) before setting off to explore the jaw-dropping Dolomites. In just half an hour, you'll be driving through pine-forested mountains.
*Follow the A22 north towards Brennero (Brenner Pass). After you see Castelrotto on a hill on the right, turn right (east) onto the SS48 towards Val Gardena.*

## 2 Ortisei (Saint Ulrich)

On the way to this pretty Alpine town, famous for its woodcarving, you'll pass deep-green meadows dotted with wildflowers, ramshackle stone farmhouses, and white churches topped with red-tiled, onion-shaped domes. At Ortisei breathe in the fresh mountain air and photograph the lovely wooden chalets on the mountain slope.
*Continue along the SS48.*

## 3 Selva di Val Gardena

As you approach Santa Cristina, the craggy Grupo del Sella mountains come into view. It's a dramatic and surreal sight at first, which is more astonishing at every turn. La Val, at the base of the awesome Selvia di Val Gardena, has a good array of accommodation, making it a great base for walks.
*Turn left towards Corvara in Badia.*

## 4 Colfosco

Colfosco, at an altitude of 1,645m (5,397ft), is surrounded by mountains: the Gruppo del Sella on one side, at 3,152m (10,341ft), with the mighty Marmolada behind at 3,342m (10,965ft), and the 'smaller' mountains of Sas Ciampac at 2,672m (8,766ft) and Sassongher at 2,665m (8,743ft) on the other side. In winter it's a snowy wonderland, but in spring and summer the fields are blanketed with wildflowers. You'll notice the temperature has dropped rapidly, even in summer.
*Continue towards Corvara in Badia.*

## 5 Corvara in Badia

Located in a big sunny basin at the foot of majestic Sassongher Mountain, Corvara is scenically sited and makes another great base for exploring the area. There is a chair lift to Piz de Lech (2,915m/9,564ft).

*Continue to wind your way through these stunning mountains, following the signs for Cortina d'Ampezzo.*

## 6 Cortina d'Ampezzo

Stretch your legs and enjoy a hot chocolate as you explore the cobblestone streets of Cortina, the jewel in the Dolomites' crown (*see also pp116–17*).

*It's hard to resist driving back the way you came, but a route north makes a nice change. Follow the signs for Dobbiaco.*

## 7 Val di Landro

This pristine area of wooden forests and serene jade-coloured lakes sees mainly Austrians and Italians coming for the cross-country skiing. Lago Dobbiaco and Lago di Landro, at the base of a craggy mountain, are simply stunning.

*At Dobbiaco turn left and follow the E66 via Brunico to meet up with the A22/E45 where you'll take the turn-off to Bressanone.*

## 8 Bressanone (Brixen)

Bend and stretch at medieval Bressanone and take a stroll around the compact historic centre and see the 13th-century Duomo (*see also p116*).

*Continue along the A22/E45 to Bolzano.*

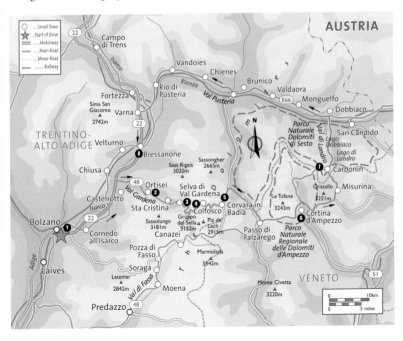

# Getting away from it all

*Northern Italy is home to some of the country's most industrialised and populated regions yet it takes little effort to get away from it all. The north boasts an excellent network of motorways, but pristine national parks, high-altitude resorts, easy hiking trails, and laid-back fishing villages are never far from the motorway exits.*

To beat the crowds, take the back roads instead of the motorways; the smaller the line on the map the greater the chance you have of being alone. Avoid visiting Northern Italy in summer

Grande Strada delle Dolomiti

when even the smallest coastal village will be crammed with tourists, especially in August. Stay clear of motorways on weekends, especially on Friday afternoons and Sunday evenings when Italians are heading to and from their weekends away.

If you are renting a car, make sure that it has 'get-up-and-go'. It needs to be powerful because you're certain to encounter winding roads with steep gradients and sharp corners. It also needs to be small because it's not uncommon for two-lane roads to turn into one-way alleys, whether the route takes you through mountains or medieval villages. Once in an historic centre, there's certain to be a few tight squeezes and it will be next to impossible to turn around a large car if you get in a traffic jam. Amateur photographers will appreciate a compact vehicle when they want to pull over on a narrow road high in the mountains to capture that postcard-perfect snap.

Parco Nazionale della Val Grande

## National parks and mountains

If you are a lover of the outdoors, the national parks and mountains of Northern Italy will provide you with a range of activities all year round.

The mountain meadows are vivid with wildflowers in spring, while the trees glow with golden leaves in autumn. In winter, snow sports such as skiing, snowboarding and mountain-climbing are popular, while in summer the hills are alive with hikers and cyclists. Walking is indeed one of the most invigorating pursuits of the region. Set out on foot on an organised hike (available through tourist offices) or self-guided on signposted walking routes with good maps and itineraries (also obtainable from tourist offices).

You can also join a guided horseback or mountain-bike excursion, or hire a personal guide to escort you.

Northern Italy's national parks see few foreign tourists compared to Italians on their country roads, walking trails and mountain climbs. The north boasts dozens of national parks, with the main parks of interest being Parco Nazionale del Gran Paradiso (Grand Paradise National Park, *see pp34–5*) and Parco Nazionale della Val Grande (Great Valley National Park) in Piemonte, and, in the Dolomites, the Parco Naturale Dolomiti di Sesto (Dolomites Nature Park), Parco Naturale Regionale delle Dolomiti d'Ampezzo (Regional Nature Park of the Dolomites of Ampezzo) and Parco Naturale Olde (Old Nature Park) in Trentino-Alto Adige.

While the Great Valley National Park itself is a delight to explore, there is also a wonderful drive around the park. The best place to set off is the turn-off at the start of the route, west of Cannobio on Lago Maggiore, which enters a wild landscape of high mountains and thick wooded forests. This narrow road slims down to a skinny single lane in parts as it snakes through the mountains, tunnelling through canopies of trees and creeping over old bridges, eventually meeting up with a main road at Malesco and the motorway at Domodossola, but it's much more fun to stay on the smaller country roads, which eventually return to Lago Maggiore, Verbania and Cannobio.

Barolo wine is produced in the hills around Alba

## Off the beaten track

Travellers determined to get away from it all should definitely hire a car for some driving tours in remote areas. Because the majority of independent foreign travellers use trains to get around, you'll find yourself among locals as you explore the back roads of Northern Italy.

There are a number of scenic routes you can enjoy in Northern Italy where you won't see another vehicle for ages, even in well-traversed regions. The trick is to avoid the motorways and use the back roads.

### Around Alba

While most visitors focus their sight-seeing on the gastronomic centres of Asti and Alba, famous for their wine and truffles, the hills south of Alba are easily worth a few hours (or at most a day) of your time. The narrow roads and lanes meander through countryside that is lush and green, and aside from the vineyards, the vegetation is wild.

The area is dotted with imposing castles and manor houses, quaint churches and crumbling farmhouses that will have you jotting down the numbers on the 'For Sale' signs. You'll also find Barolo in this area, famous for its robust red wines. While there are a number of signposted wine routes you can follow, with cellar doors where you can taste and purchase wine, it's more fun to take a map and chart your own routes through this very scenic part of Northern Italy.

### Camogli

Some of Northern Italy's most off-the-beaten-track villages are in spitting distance of towns popular with tourists, yet due to their lack of English media exposure they may be unknown to foreigners. Not all of them are engaging enough to warrant an overnight stay yet they are worth dropping into if you're in the area. Some, in turn, might boast few attractions yet are rewarding places to spend a few days exploring, and ideal if you're looking to do nothing more than relax.

A good example is the charming fishing village Camogli, just 20km

(12½ miles) northeast of Portofino, with its pretty pastel-coloured buildings. Crammed with Italians in summer, Camogli sees comparatively few foreign tourists, and even fewer choosing to check in somewhere and stay awhile. With the Cinque Terre villages becoming uncomfortably over-crowded and Portofino already over-priced, Camogli makes a more authentic and affordable alternative (*see also p50*).

## Cinque Terre

Not far from Camogli, Cinque Terre is one of Italy's most beautiful and most visited areas, yet most people take the train between towns. This is because good roads have only connected the villages in recent years – and prior to their development the routes were nothing more than donkey tracks – and many guidebooks still claim it's impossible to drive between some of the villages.

However, you can, and you will be rewarded with some of Italy's most spectacular views of the coastline, sea and villages. While the route can be done in a few hours, allow a full day if you plan to spend time exploring each village and enjoying lunch, coffee and ice-cream stops on the way.

*Getting away from it all*

Villa Rosmarino is a good place to stay if you are exploring the Camogli area

Alternatively, break the journey in two and check into a hotel for the night halfway at Corniglia. Start at Levanto in the north of Cinque Terre and follow the route along the coast in a southeasterly direction, or begin at La Spezia or Portovenere in the south and head northwest – many locals prefer driving the latter direction in the late afternoon (*see pp54–5*).

It's an edge-of-your-seat experience as the road twists and turns while it snakes around the hills, clinging somewhat precariously to the mountains in parts. Take care with switchbacks and hug the hillside when you can – although in some places you won't have a choice, as it's extremely narrow in sections.

The winding Cinque Terre coast road will test your driving skills

Keep in mind you cannot drive into the heart of the villages, which often have narrow cobblestone streets, but each has a car park on the edge of town. However, you may have to walk for some distance to reach the centre of the village, so if you're staying overnight contact your hotel in advance if you need help with luggage.

Avoid driving between villages at weekends and during the warm summer months when Italians like to do the drive and swim at the village beaches and it can be impossible to park close to town – you'll probably find yourself parking at the top of a hill and walking down, and while you can enjoy the views on your way, after a long lunch you'll be dreading the sweltering hike back up.

### Via Aurelia: Sanremo to the French Border

Visitors driving between France and Italy along the Mediterranean tend to zip along the A1 *autostrada*, yet more enjoyable than the motorway is the SS1 or Via Aurelia, which follows an ancient Roman trading route. The drive follows the slower jagged route Riviera di Ponente seaboard from Sanremo to Menton on the French border, snaking through pretty towns precariously perched on mountains, vineyards growing on steep hillsides, and verdant gardens tucked into valleys.

Via Aurelia zigzags through the seaside towns of Ospedaletti, Bordighera, Vallecrosia and Ventimiglia, all of which have a rather ramshackle feel to them,

Corniglia is stunningly beautiful

despite boasting elegant villas and grand apartment buildings. The towns have an authenticity you won't find in many Italian seaside resorts. They also have a more laid-back atmosphere compared to east-coast resorts such as Rimini, which are popular with young clubbers and big families. This is mainly because many of the Riviera di Ponente residents are retirees enjoying the sunshine and slow pace of life.

Closer to the French border, the towns get more sophisticated and gentrified, the architecture of the buildings more refined, and their gardens become neater. From here it's a short drive to ritzy Monte Carlo, which, while hardly 'off the beaten track' sees few foreign tourists visiting from Italy but is certainly worth a look if you're not planning to rush back to France.

# When to go

*Northern Italy has a generally mild climate with a moderate chance of rain right through the year. The winters can be cold and the height of summer hot and muggy, making spring and autumn the best times to visit. Or just act like a local and head to the lakes for summer and the mountains for winter. On average, the hottest month is July and the coldest January, with November having the most rain.*

Spring is the best time to visit if you're on a sightseeing trip around the towns and cities of the region. The temperatures are pleasant – if a little cool in March – and rainfall is relatively infrequent. As winter finally thaws out, the region really comes alive again – and Italians love being *alfresco*! As many of the places to visit are best done on foot, this is a fine time to be in the North. This time of year also avoids key holiday seasons and is a shoulder travel season, so popular destinations such as Venice are not overcrowded.

While early June is fine, once high season starts (around mid-month) the temperature and the number of tourists increase quickly. Many of the cities on travel agendas (such as Milan, Genova and Venice) can be uncomfortably humid. As the humidity arrives, the attention in the North turns to the lakes and beaches and literally everyone in Italy has August off – either physically or mentally! Many fine restaurants and shops are shut during

the month and it's generally good advice not to spend August *anywhere* in Italy except lying on the beach with a paperback in hand.

Once the Italians head back to work tanned and refreshed and the summer hordes have departed, it's a good time

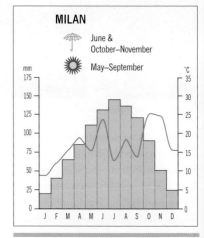

**WEATHER CONVERSION CHART**

25.4mm = 1 inch

°F = 1.8 × °C + 32

Portofino's summer weather attracts visiting celebrities

to travel in the North. It's still warm and you can still swim in the lakes comfortably in September, and the rainfall is low enough until November. As it's a shoulder season, bookings are easier to come by and hotels are generally not charging the rate they did during summer. November, however, is the wettest month of the year, and while it becomes miserable in cities such as Milan, Venice suffers from the *acqua alte* (high water) that floods the city, making sightseeing rather uncomfortable.

While it can be dreary in many towns in the North during winter, the upside is that the ski resorts and charming mountain towns are buzzing. From late December to mid-March the mountains are the place to steal away to. Many places on the lakes will have very few tourists and only Milan, Venice and Turin have a significant tourism presence – apart from the winter resorts. Still, the upside of winter in the North is all that lovely rustic food that Italians do so well!

# Getting around

*Northern Italy is best explored by car. The most convenient way is to fly into Milan and pick up a hire car to explore the lakes and mountains at your leisure, perhaps dropping off the car at Venice before flying out. While there is plenty of twisting terrain to cover – which is half the fun of Northern Italian driving – the* autostrade *make covering long distances a breeze. Train travel is also a good way to explore, but you'll miss some of the amazing scenery.*

## By air

Foreign visitors do not typically journey by air within Italy. Domestic travel tends to be the domain of Italians and business travellers. Train travel is a much more popular way to move between major cities with fast trains connecting them. There are flights between major cities such as Milan, Turin, Venice, Verona and Bologna in the north, and southern cities such as Rome, Naples, Palermo and Catania, with airlines such as Alitalia (*www.alitalia.com*), Meridiana (*www.meridiana.it*) and My Air (*www.myair.com*).

## By car

It's always best to book car hire in advance, as cars in each category are often thin on the ground. Also, booking your car with your flight is often a good way to get a discounted daily rate. EU licensed drivers need only their current driver's licence. Drivers from other countries need to check with the rental agency as often an International Driving Permit is required. This is usually available through your local automobile club.

### Driving conditions

The roads of Northern Italy are generally in great shape. The *autostrada* A4 runs from Turin across Northern Italy to Venice and allows you to cover great distances quickly. Minor roads zigzag their way through the mountainous regions and, while picturesque, should be tackled in small doses – in no small part because of the locals' habit of choosing the best line through twisting roads rather than sticking to their own side of the road. Ensure that your hire car has a working horn. If you are heading into the mountains, choose a vehicle with decent horsepower, but keep in mind that a small narrow car is better to navigate the lake roads and mountain passes. If you're heading into the mountains in winter, be sure to have a set of snow chains included in your rental package.

**Road rules**

In Italy you drive on the right side of the road. When on an *autostrada*, keep to the right to allow faster vehicles to pass on the left. This will happen frequently! Unless you are on a roundabout (those already on the roundabout have right of way), vehicles on your right have right of way. Speed limits are 130km/h (80mph) on the *autostrade* 110 km/h (68mph) on main roads, 90km/h (56mph) on rural roads and 50km/h (31mph) through residential areas. The blood-alcohol content limit is 0.5gr.

**By train**

Train travel is a common means of transport in Italy and indeed a straight journey from Venice to Milan is often quicker by train than flying – especially when you take into account the extra airport waiting times, transfer times, and

Milan has an extensive tram network

hoping that your luggage flops out on to the carousel. There are stops right across the region, and indeed in some cities and towns not having a car to park is a distinctly advantageous way to travel. The only real downside is that there is the occasional train strike, so always confirm that the trains are running before heading to the station – just in case – with Trenitalia (*www.trenitalia.com*).

If you are travelling exclusively and extensively by train, you may wish to consider purchasing a Trenitalia pass.

**By public transport**

One of the joys of travelling in Italy and exploring its historic cities, compared to cities such as London, New York or Sydney, is the ability to get everywhere on foot and stroll along traffic-free, cobblestone streets. When your legs do tire, however, there is often a bus, or in cities such as Milan, a tram or underground train, to take you somewhere. The only cities in which you may find yourself wanting to ride public transport are Milan, Genova, Turin and Venice, and this is probably only if you find yourself staying outside the historic centre (something travellers rarely do). In this case, before leaving the hotel, find out what forms of transport will bring you closest to the hotel and jot down the route number. Bus, train and tram systems within cities are managed locally, so pick up a timetable from the local tourist office if you are staying for any length of time.

# Accommodation

*As you would expect for such a design-focused region of Italy, there are some slick, minimalist city hotels in the region, particularly in Milan, Genova and Turin. On the lakes there are some wonderful 'grand old piles' that transport guests to another era, and some fascinating oddities, such as the Moorish Villa Crespi at Lago d'Orta. There is certainly enough variety in accommodation to gratify everyone, including those with a penchant for in-room espresso machines and staff in designer uniforms.*

Italy's star classification system is similar to other countries in Europe in terms of facilities and amenity levels, but the level of service is a little more erratic than most. Often a family-run three-star can have better personal service than a five-star luxury hotel; however, some small hotels treat guests as an unwelcome interruption to a football match that's playing on the TV. The Italian word *albergo* simply means hotel, while a *locanda* is generally a small hotel in the shape of a set of rooms converted to hotel accommodation within a large house. *Pensiones* still exist, although many of these are now one- or two-star properties. The classification *Bed and Breakfast* can simply mean what it says, or it can be a charming establishment that has more atmosphere than an international chain hotel can muster. Along those lines, the *agriturismo* trend is becoming very popular in Italy, where visitors stay on a property in the country or a working farm. The execution of this can be hit-or-miss,

though (see *www.loveitaly.co.uk* or *www.agriturist.it* for more information).

Many national parks and mountain areas are peppered with cosy wooden cabins and B&Bs, grand hotels with fireplaces and sweeping staircases, and heavenly mountain resorts where you'll literally have your head in the clouds. A stay here can be as relaxing as it can be invigorating, especially if combined with Nordic walking and spa treatments. Local tourist offices have long lists of unique accommodation options on offer, such as Vigilius (*see p173*), a high-altitude mountain resort on Vigiljoch Mountain near Lana that has to be visited to be believed.

If you wish to stay longer than a few days in Turin, renting an apartment is more economical and more fun. Rentxpress (*www.rentxpress.com*) has some stylish properties in good locations around the city.

Something to be aware of while visiting Northern Italy is that for those who need to do business while

Grand Hotel Villa Serbelloni defines old-school elegance on Lake Como

travelling, your best bet is the upmarket chains, which will have a functioning business centre and useable internet. Elsewhere internet access is sporadic at the best of times, and expensive. A hotel with a garage can be a real plus if you're looking to stay in the centre of a city such as Verona.

Check-in and check-out times can vary dramatically, with some boutique hotels having a decidedly guest-unfriendly 10am check-out. If you're staying on the lakes or in the mountains, a room with a view is distinctly more romantic, and while you will pay for it, sipping a glass of something bubbly while taking in the vista might be one of your best experiences on the trip.

May through to September are the busiest months, with July and August the real high season. The exception is the mountain ski resorts such as Cortina d'Ampezzo, where occupancy is at its highest from Christmas through to late March. Booking is essential at these times. Travelling in the off-season or shoulder season gives you more flexibility both with room rates and with your itinerary, especially when the shopping in Milan or the restaurants on the lakes beckon you to extend that extra day or two.

The prices in Northern Italy can vary wildly. In some cities, such as Turin, a five-star hotel might have the same rate as a three-star in a ski resort, while in others, such as Venice, a one-star can go for the price of a four-star in Genova. Some hotels have set tariffs and discounts during shoulder and low periods, while others have different rates for the different seasons.

# Food and drink

*The food and wine of the North would make a trip to this region worth it even without taking in the sights! From the humble old staple polenta (cornmeal), served in a modest osteria (a wine and food 'inn') to the coveted white truffles of Alba shaved onto your dish at a world-renowned restaurant, the North is a gastronomic delight. The wines of the region are wonderful as well, each geographic area having a distinctive wine or two that tempt the taste buds (see pp38–9).*

Milan has a wonderful gastronomic tradition, with dishes such as *Cotoletta Milanese* (veal cutlets) recalling the reign of the Austrians in its similarity to *Wiener schnitzel*. *Ossobucco*, braised veal shanks, is another Milanese favourite and is often served with *Risotto alla Milanese*, slow-cooked rice with saffron threads.

As you travel through the North, you'll notice that each region and city has its classic dishes or ingredients that play a major role in Italy's wonderful cuisine. For instance, Parma has its renowned Parma hams and Parmigiano-Reggiano, the king of cheeses. Bologna has *Ragù alla Bolognese* (Bolognese sauce) and Mortadella sausage, while Modena is famous for its *Aceto Balsamico Tradizionale*, balsamic vinegar. The list and the flavours are endless. Don't miss the opportunity to try these celebrated ingredients and dishes where they originated from. And of course, match local wines to whatever you eat!

## Vegetarian options

Vegetarians eat well in Italy, with plenty of meat-free pizza and pasta dishes that are just as tasty as the ones that contain *carne* (meat). Grilled vegetables and salads, as well as bean dishes, are also delicious in Italy; however, vegans will find it harder-going.

## Meal times

Breakfast (*la colazione*) is generally from 7 until 10.30am, but if you're looking for a café at 7am you'll be lucky to find a warm coffee machine in town. As Italians generally have a light breakfast – usually a pastry such as a *cornetto* (croissant) and a coffee – you won't find much more than this on offer in all but the top-end hotels. Lunch (*il pranzo*) generally runs from noon until 2pm, although in seaside resorts they may take orders until 3pm. For many locals, this is the big meal of the day (it certainly is on weekends), consisting of at least two courses.

Dinner (*la cena*) is generally from 7–7.30pm until 10–10.30pm and is usually a couple of courses.

## Types of eatery

Typically, a *ristorante* is the most elegant and expensive of Italy's eateries and a *trattoria* is a more casual version of a *ristorante*; both are generally open for lunch and dinner. An *osteria* is a small eatery, quite often only open for dinner, and an *enoteca* is a wine bar usually open at the owner's whim, but always in the evening.

A jacket is generally not required, although most Italian men will don one. It's always best to book ahead if there's more than four in your party.

## The menu

You'll often find the menu split up into several courses. You might be offered an apertif such as Campari to start off with, or some *prosecco* (sparkling wine). The first course is *antipasto* (literally meaning 'before the meal'). This usually consists of items such as cured meats and cheeses or *bruschetta* (toasted bread with olive oil and various toppings). *Primo* is literally the first course and usually consists of pasta or risotto or a hearty soup. *Secondo* (second course) is the main dish, usually locally caught fish or meat. As the meat or fish dish is often served without any extra vegetables, a *contorno*, or side dish, of cooked vegetables is usually available, too. A cheese (*formaggio*) course may be offered next, before *dolce* (dessert), *caffè*

A mixed plate of cold meats is typical *antipasto*

(coffee) and a *digestivo* (a shot of liqueur such as *grappa* or *limoncello*), which, if you've managed to get through all those courses, will probably be on the house!

## Tipping

You will often find a cover charge (*coperto*), generally one or two euros, on *il conto* (the bill). This is for water and bread: it is not a tip. If *servizio* is included on the total, no tipping is necessary, otherwise tip up to 10 per cent for good service.

## Shopping and markets

Food and wine shopping is first class in the North. In Milan, **Peck** (*Via Hugo Victor 4, Milan; tel: (02) 861 040; www.peck.it*) is widely considered to be the best delicatessen in Italy. Local markets and delicatessens in the smaller towns are renowned for their quality and you can pick up a great selection of salamis, cheeses and breads. Seasonal fruits and vegetables are sold everywhere from a roadside stall to markets in town squares.

# Entertainment

*Northern Italy is a refined destination when it comes to entertainment, with Milan heading the charge when it comes to opera, classical, jazz and pop music. Its bars and clubs shine as well, but cities such as Genova, Turin, Venice and Verona also know how to put on a sophisticated show but still let their hair down – when the time is right.*

## Classical music

Your chances of catching a classical music performance are good in Northern Italy. Milan has a symphony season at La Scala and the well-regarded Orchestra Sinfonica di Milano Giuseppe Verdi has its home at the Auditorium of Milan. Various other multipurpose venues around the city often host concerts as well.

Turin has an enviable reputation for classical music, with the highly respected RAI Orchestra Sinfonica Nazionale (National Symphony Orchestra) having its home there, as well as its own auditorium where its winter symphonic season (October to May) is a must-do. The Lingotto Auditorium, designed by famous architect Renzo Piano, has a full calendar of events, and the ever-present Giuseppe Verdi has a conservatory named after him, which holds chamber music recitals. Venice has many concerts in its various churches (heavy on Vivaldi – always a crowd-pleaser), as does Verona.

## Opera

Milan and opera go together like a hand in a bespoke glove. What can one say about an opera theatre where Giuseppe Verdi was once house composer, Rossini and Puccini premiered some of their best works, and Maria Callas was a constant artistic presence during the height of her career? La Scala is simply one of the best opera houses in the world and its restored splendour is a must-see for anyone who has even a passing interest in opera. But opera is not just confined to Milan, for Verdi and Callas were also visible throughout the rest of Northern Italy; Callas performed at the breathtaking outdoor Arena di Verona in the early years of her career and had a career turning point at the Venice's Teatro la Fenice, where Verdi had premiered his masterpiece opera *Rigoletto* in 1851.

## Jazz

Italy has been a hotbed of jazz since the end of World War I and nearly every city in the North has a club devoted to jazz and live performances. Enrico Rava, a jazz trumpeter, is probably Italy's best-known jazz musician. Milan is arguably the home of jazz in the North with several good venues, including a Blue Note club that has the most kudos. Genova and Bologna have solid jazz scenes.

## Pop and rock

Milan is definitely the centre of pop and rock music in the North. It's on the circuit for European tours for any big band, especially when they visit Europe for the summer festivals. Well-known bands tend to play at the Forum, the Stadio Meazza (San Siro) football stadium or Mazda Palace, while mid-sized acts opt for venues such as Alcatraz, Magazzini Generali or Rolling Stone. The best way to find out what is coming up (besides using the internet) is at the various music stores in town, such as Messaggerie Musicali, which has a box office as well as stocking free local magazines and booklets that have concert details in them. Other cities and towns will often have one-off musical events, held, for example, at the Arena di Verona, which boasts a busy summer concert schedule.

## Cinema

Despite the long relationship between film and Northern Italy, the irony is that while the Venice Film Festival is one of the most prestigious festivals in the world, at present there is only one cinema venue left in Venice! Things are much better in Milan, which has an

The fully restored Teatro alla Scala

enormous number of cinemas playing mainly Italian first-run features, neither dubbed into English nor with any subtitles. Many cinemas do have recent Hollywood releases, but these are generally dubbed instead of subtitled.

## Bars and clubs

The bar scene is excellent in Milan, especially if you take into account the *aperitivo* hour (*see box p69*). To see Milan's bar culture in full swing, head to the Navigli and Porta Ticinese on a Friday or Saturday night. Other cities of the North have similar scenes, notably Genova, Turin and Parma.

Clubs are generally empty until midnight and close around 4am. Often the cover charge is steep, but includes a free drink or two. The music is generally eclectic – ranging from hip-hop to cheesy pop to retro happy house music – so choose your nights carefully.

# Shopping

*One of the delights of travelling through Northern Italy is the superlative shopping in the region. Every big city, town and village boasts an attractive central piazza and cobblestone pedestrian streets, lined with elegant shops with beautifully designed window displays. From exclusive fashion, handmade gloves and hats in Milan to silk ties and leather bags in Como, from extravagantly painted masks and vibrant-coloured Murano glass in Venice to sleek furniture and playful kitchen utensils from Alessi, Northern Italy has it all.*

## Fashion and accessories

There's no denying Milan is a shopping Mecca, but as one of the great fashion capitals of the world, alongside Paris, London and New York, it is a paradise for fashionistas. Whether you're after the latest designer fashions (literally straight off the catwalk), vintage couture, finely crafted leather shoes, handbags and belts, bespoke hats and gloves, or contemporary jewellery, you'll find it in Milan – you'll also discover gorgeous little shops specialising in everything from antique glassware to recycled stationery. All the big names of Italian fashion are here, including Versace, Prada, Gucci, Dolce&Gabbana, Missoni, Moschino, Valentino, Mariella Burani and Gianfranco Ferre. Giorgio Armani's sleek designer department store is nearby and is a must-visit.

As you travel around Northern Italy, you'll see many of these same designers, along with Italian high-street fashion franchises, such as Benetton and Sisley, in Como, Turin, Genova, Parma, Modena, Bologna, Ravenna, Verona and Venice. But the same cities are also home to delightful, old-fashioned stores such as Sermoneta, the handmade leather glovemakers (in Milan and Venice), and Borsalino (in Milan, Como and Parma), where you can buy a fine Panama hat to wear for boating on the lakes. Famous for its silk, Como's quaint cobbled streets are home to charming stores selling scarves, ties and shawls.

Fake glasses and handbags are ubiquitous in Italy, as they are all over Europe. Remember that you'll only buy a true Gucci bag in a Gucci shop, or from an authorised distributor of Gucci products.

## Design

After fashion, Northern Italy is best known for its contemporary design. While Milan has long been Italy's design centre, Turin, renowned for its automobile industry, has in recent years wrested the title of design capital from Milan. The Lakes area, where many of the manufacturers are, is the spot to head for chic furniture, home décor and kitchenware; however, you'll find stylish design stores in all of Northern Italy's cities and towns. Names to watch for include Alessi, whose headquarters and factory are on Lago Como; Kartell, the Milanese pioneer of plastic (the flagship store is in Milan), and Momo Design, makers of hip motorcycle helmets, sunglasses, torches, driving gloves and accessories for motoring enthusiasts. At **SAG '80** (*Via Boccaccio 4, Milan. Tel: (02) 481 5380*), you'll find all the big names: Artemide, B&B Italia, Boffi, Cappellini, Dada, Driade, Flos, Knoll, Matteograssi, Minotti, Vitra and Zanotta.

Galleria Vittorio Emanuele II in Milan has many designer shops

## Fine food and wine

Some of the best souvenirs you can buy in Italy are edible ones – provided your country's customs authority allows you to take them home. Vacuum-packed cheeses and cured meats cost a fraction of the price here and it will have you fondly recalling your trip as you slice another piece of *prosciutto* months later. Alternatively, buy a bottle of locally pressed olive oil or a jar of truffle picker's paste, which you might not be able to buy where you live. Bologna, Turin, Genova, Parma and Modena are all great food cities with fantastic shops, but Milan is probably the gourmet capital with a few must-visit gastronomic stores.

## Markets

Most Northern Italian cities and towns hold weekly markets, where you can buy clothes, books and records, and even antiques and bric-a-brac. Some

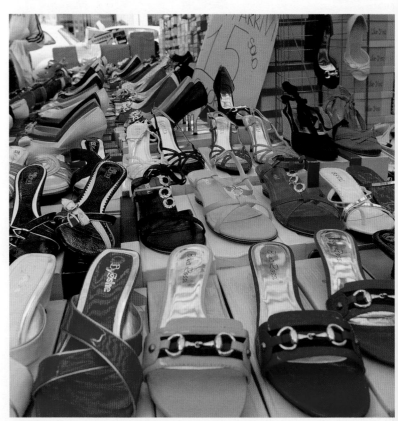

Viale Papiniano market is popular with bargain fashion shoppers

will have a monthly antiques and art fair that rocks up to town, often on a Sunday, and takes over the piazza or pedestrian shopping street. There will also be a fresh produce market where you can buy locally grown seasonal fruit and vegetables, seafood, meat, wine, cheeses and cold cuts. These are great places to head for picnic supplies, such as hot chickens, fresh breads, olives and antipasto. They're generally held once a week and open all day, although the best time to go may be first thing in the morning; ask your hotel or the local tourist office.

The best markets in Milan include a fascinating flea market on Saturdays on Viale Gabriele d'Annunzio; a popular food, clothes and plants market on Tuesday and Saturday mornings on Viale Papiniano; an antiques and second-hand market on the last Sunday of each month on the Naviglio Grande and Ripa di Porta Ticinese; and an antiques market every third Saturday of the month on Via Fiori Chiari in the Brera. Antiques shops and art galleries also line the Naviglio, the streets of the Brera on Via Brera and Solferino, and around Sant'Ambrogio, on San Maurilio and Via San Giovani.

In Turin, the sprawling Balon Flea Market on Saturdays on Piazza Repubblica is famous throughout Italy for its bargain-basement clothes and textiles, and fresh produce. On the second Sunday of the month there is an antiques market in the same location. In Venice, the daily Rialto market is one of Italy's best fresh food markets with superb seafood straight from the sea and the finest-quality fruit and vegetables. The market is reason enough to have a self-catering holiday in Venice. There are some wonderful cheese shops in the surrounding lanes, and of course the souvenir stalls leading to and over the Rialto Bridge.

## Department stores

Don't expect to see department stores in every city and town. Italians prefer small, specialised shops, because the service is more attentive, professional, knowledgeable and personal, and they know where the products are from or if they don't they can find out. The two main department stores are La Rinascente and Coin, and you'll find these in most towns. The stores in Milan are the most impressive. Giorgio Armani actually dressed the windows of Milan's La Rinascente in the 1960s!

## Books, films and music

Italian films and music make fabulous souvenirs. Your first stop should be Messaggerie Musicali and Ricordi Media Stores, two of Italy's biggest franchises for books, CDs and DVDs, with stores in most big towns. They have an unrivalled range of beautiful coffee-table books on Italy, Italian cookbooks, Italian literature and English-language novels. Italian Touring Club bookshops are your best bet for travel guidebooks, maps, dictionaries and phrase books, and they have branches in Milan, Turin and Genova.

# Sport and leisure

*Northern Italians love the great outdoors and keeping fit, and the mountains and lakes offer seasonally focused sports from sailing in summer to snowboarding in winter. Spectator sports are popular as well; the region boasts some of Italy's best football teams and is the spiritual home of all forms of motor sports.*

### Cycling

All forms of cycling are popular in Northern Italy. Summer sees the trend of turning ski lifts into lifts for mountain bikers in resorts such as Bardonecchia near Turin, while road racers punish their lycra-clad legs with mountain hill climbs all over the North. For a more relaxed two-wheeled adventure, the lakes are fun to circumnavigate and there are guides as well as decent bikes to rent on the popular lakes.

### Football

Northern Italy currently boasts half of the football (soccer) teams competing in Serie A, Italy's Premier League, considered one of the elite leagues in the world. Several of these teams have been some of Serie A's consistent performers: Inter Milan, AC Milan, Turin's Juventus and Torino FC. Other teams currently in Serie A from Northern Italy are AC Chievo Verona, Genova's Genoa CFC and UC

Sampdoria, Bologna FC, Bergamo's Atalanta BC, and Udinese Calcio, based in Udine, Friuli-Venezia Giulia.

While a match featuring any of these sides is worth attending, matches between Inter Milan and AC Milan (called the 'Derby della Madonnina') and Inter Milan and Juventus (dubbed the 'Derby d'Italia') are highlights of any season. A match at Milan's famous San Siro stadium is also a highlight for football lovers.

### Golf

While there are several golf clubs in Milan's environs, most visitors opt for rounds on courses near the lakes such as Lago Como, Lago di Garda and Lago d'Iseo. Many of these courses are open in the warmer months only.

### Hiking and climbing

Hiking is very popular in Northern Italy – some would say a little too popular in the Cinque Terre during the warmer months. The walk between the five villages of Monterosso, Vernazza, Corniglia, Manarola and Riomaggiore around the coastline is stunning and perhaps the most popular hiking route in Italy. As a result, it gets very crowded.

Popular hiking areas in the mountains include the Dolomites around Cortina d'Ampezzo. Climbing is also popular during the warmer months at the resorts of Cortina d'Ampezzo and Courmayeur, and the famous climbing region of Valle d'Aosta, considered the home of modern mountaineering. These renowned resorts have excellent English-speaking local guides who are used to accommodating all levels of climbers.

## Horse riding

Lago Maggiore and Lago Como are popular destinations for horse riding in Northern Italy, with the hills and lakes offering wonderful vistas as well as interesting riding. English-speaking guides and itineraries for novices or experienced riders are available.

Sport and leisure

Hiring a bike for a lake excursion is popular

## Motor racing

With Northern Italy being the home of sports car manufacturer Ferrari (in Modena), Ducati motorcycles (in Bologna) and Moto Guzzi (Lake Como) amongst others, it's natural that the region is a Mecca for motor sport lovers. While a visit to the Ferrari museum is a must (*see p62*), the Italian Formula One Grand Prix held at Monza in mid-September is an equally compelling draw for motor sports enthusiasts. One of the longest-running events on the motor sports calendar, it's always an exciting race on one of the world's most celebrated tracks. Indeed

Canoeing on Lago d'Orta

the Italians call it 'La Pista Magica' – the magic track. The rest of the year sees a pretty full calendar of events here, and at certain times you can even do some laps there in your hire car – just don't tell the rental company! On occasion testing is open to the public as well, and when you visit the Ferrari Museum you can sometimes hear the buzz of Formula One cars blasting around Fiorina circuit down the road, where you might catch a glimpse of the 'Prancing Horses' being tested through the fence.

## Watersports
### Sailing and canoeing
Every lake in Northern Italy that's big enough to float a boat has rental boats of many varieties. You can rent everything from a *barca a vela* (sailing boat) to a *motoscafo* (motor boat). The more popular areas, such as the north end of Lago di Garda, have businesses that rent catamarans and sailboats with instructors for all levels. Keen canoeists will love exploring the lakes as well, and there are excellent canoes for hire on the lakes – as well as some that are barely seaworthy.

## Wind and kite surfing
Lake surfing is very popular in Italy and the region has some of the best conditions in Europe, with reliable thermal winds (both in the early morning and late afternoon) and magnificent surroundings. The north ends of the lakes have the best conditions, and Lakes Garda, Como and Iseo are popular, with Lake Garda having the most extensive facilities. Lessons as well as good equipment are for hire here.

## Winter sports
Come December in Northern Italy, it's not just Santa the locals are looking forward to, they're praying for a white Christmas as well. While Northern Italians will spend most of August working on their tan, they'll spend at least a full week in winter working on their turns at their favourite ski resort. The tradition of the *settimana bianca* (white week) is strong here, and with the large number of resorts everyone has a favourite. There are two main regions for winter sports, Valle d'Aosta and the Dolomites. Valle d'Aosta is in the northwest corner of Italy, with Switzerland to the north and France to the west. The Matterhorn, Monte Gran Paradiso, Monte Rosa and Monte Bianco (Mont Blanc, Europe's tallest peak) are all here and the resort of Courmayeur is perhaps the best-known winter resort, with Turin, in the neighbouring region of Piemonte, being the largest city nearby. The other famous winter sports region is the Dolomites, with both the chic Cortina d'Ampezzo and more youthful Madonna di Campiglio as key resorts. The snow is usually better later in the season (which generally extends from mid-December to late March). If you're driving, remember those snow chains.

# Children

*While the gastronomy, opera, shopping and art museums of Northern Italy might be trying for the little ones, summer on the lakes or winter in the mountains are perfect for a family break. Italians love children and they are well catered for in the popular holiday destinations of the region.*

Cafés and restaurants in Northern Italy are well used to catering for kids and they are generally welcomed with open arms. The more popular holiday spots will have children's menus, or at least offer a half-portion of simple dishes such as pasta, and a couple of scoops of *gelato* (ice cream) can keep even the most hyperactive child (and adult!) quiet for a few minutes. Northern Italy has wonderful parks, delicatessens and markets, so picnics are a great idea for families. Kicking a ball around with local kids is a great way to make friends too.

Keep in mind when travelling through Northern Italy that a packed itinerary taking in several cities over a couple of weeks is generally too much for small children, especially if using public transport. Taking a car makes more sense and offers more flexibility as well as perhaps ending up being less expensive than lots of train tickets. If visiting the lakes or mountains, it's better to have a base for a few days and use the car to do day trips.

In Milan, sights such as the Museo Scienza e Della Tecnica, Teatro delle Marionette, the views from the roof of the Duomo, and Castello Sforzesco (*see pp69–75*) keep children interested and entertained. Castles are well worth visiting, as are Roman ruins. Don't forget that children get great discounts or free entry to many attractions.

In Venice, children find the pigeons on Saint Mark's Square fun and you'll probably be talked into a gondola ride! Riding the *vaporetti* 'water buses' on all the routes is a highlight, as is watching the passing water traffic from the Rialto Bridge. In Turin there is an array of fantastic interactive museums, such as the Museo Nazionale del Cinema (National Film Museum, *see pp29–30*).

On the lakes, it's easy to keep the children entertained and engaged. Besides the boat rides, canoeing and fishing, there are often cable-car or funicular rides as well as wonderful gardens to explore, often with exotic fish, turtles or birdlife.

The big tourist attraction on the lakes for children, though, is Gardaland (*see p165*), an entertainment park that caters for children – as the saying goes – of all ages. It's a massive complex, considered to be the best in Italy, and can easily swallow up a couple of days taking in all the rides. They even have their own hotel to make that easier to do!

A winter wonderland is a kids' favourite as well, and the resorts of Italy cater for children quite well. Cortina d'Ampezzo, Courmayeur and Cervinia are great choices for family ski holidays as they have good hotels for families and good facilities for beginners and children.

Don't forget when planning your trip to check for events as well, as these will often cater for children as well as adults – with bands, clowns and plenty of food. When all else fails to keep the children entertained, remember this one word of advice – *gelato*.

Messing about on the water on the Cinque Terre coast will keep children amused for hours

# Essentials

## Arriving and departing
### By air
The two main cities in the region that are international flight hubs are Milan and Venice, although low-cost airlines are taking advantage of other smaller airports in the region. Milan has two airports, **Malpensa** (*www.sea-aeroportimilano.it. Tel: (02) 7485 2200*) 45km (28 miles) from Milan city centre and **Linate** (*www.sea-aeroportimilano.it. Tel: (02) 7485 2200*) about 8km (5 miles) from the centre.

Malpensa handles the bulk of international traffic and has a 40-minute express train to Cadorna train station in Milan leaving every 15 minutes. From there you'll either have to take a taxi or brave the metro with your luggage. Note that Malpensa is halfway to the lakes, convenient if you're heading to Lago Como and its environs. Linate handles mainly domestic traffic and is a half-hour bus ride from Stazione Centrale (check notice boards for information). Buses also run regularly between the two airports.

Venice's **Marco Polo Airport** (*www.veniceairport.it. Tel: (041) 260 9260*) is on the mainland with connections by bus (Venice-Piazzale Roma terminal), train (Venice-Mestre) and – for a more fitting way to arrive in Venice – water taxi.

### By road
The most popular routes to Northern Italy for those travelling by road from neighbouring European countries are via the French Riviera and Monte Carlo to Ventimiglia, from Mont Blanc (Monte Bianco) in the north to Aosta, and via Brig in Switzerland to Domodossola, not far from Verbania. It's also possible to enter from Austria to Tarvisio and from Slovenia to Gorizia.

### By rail
You can take high-speed trains from other European capitals to Milan and Venice. In Milan, busy Stazione Centrale is four metro stops from Piazza Duomo, although if you have lots of luggage you can take a taxi – also recommended late at night – Stazione Centrale is a noted pickpockets' palace. In Venice, the train terminates at Santa Lucia station on the canals and from here it's best to know *exactly* where your lodgings are to save you from getting lost before you even dump your bags at the hotel.

## Customs
Italian customs allows a 'reasonable amount' of alcohol and tobacco products to be brought into Italy from other EU countries. From countries outside the EU, the limits are 200 cigarettes or 50 cigars, two litres of table wine or one litre of alcohol.

Essentials

## Electricity

Italy's electricity system is 220 volts. Plugs are either European two rounded or three rounded pins. UK appliances will work with an adaptor.

## Internet

Internet availability in the region is widespread and all cities and most towns will have an internet café. However, it is not as common in hotels as it is in other parts of Europe. Most five-star hotels have some form of wi-fi, although the in-room wi-fi is hit or miss – and expensive.

## Money

The currency of Italy is the euro (€), which is divided up into 100 *centesimi* (cents). Post offices offer decent exchange rates.

While the usual credit and debit cards are accepted most places, it's good to carry around some cash for small *trattorie* which may not accept cards, and for tipping. ATMs (called Bankomats) are plentiful in the region, but many of them only work with Italian cards.

Traveller's cheques are increasingly not accepted in Italy, so are best avoided.

## Opening hours

Opening hours tend to be erratic in Italy, but less so in the north. Most shops are open from 9am–noon and from 3 or 4pm until 7pm and closed on Monday mornings, and many are closed on Wednesday afternoons.

## CONVERSION TABLE

| FROM | TO | MULTIPLY BY |
|---|---|---|
| Inches | Centimetres | 2.54 |
| Feet | Metres | 0.3048 |
| Yards | Metres | 0.9144 |
| Miles | Kilometres | 1.6090 |
| Acres | Hectares | 0.4047 |
| Gallons | Litres | 4.5460 |
| Ounces | Grams | 28.35 |
| Pounds | Grams | 453.6 |
| Pounds | Kilograms | 0.4536 |
| Tons | Tonnes | 1.0160 |

To convert back, for example from centimetres to inches, divide by the number in the third column.

### MEN'S SUITS

| | | | | | | | |
|---|---|---|---|---|---|---|---|
| UK | 36 | 38 | 40 | 42 | 44 | 46 | 48 |
| Rest of Europe | 46 | 48 | 50 | 52 | 54 | 56 | 58 |
| USA | 36 | 38 | 40 | 42 | 44 | 46 | 48 |

### DRESS SIZES

| | | | | | | |
|---|---|---|---|---|---|---|
| UK | 8 | 10 | 12 | 14 | 16 | 18 |
| France | 36 | 38 | 40 | 42 | 44 | 46 |
| Italy | 38 | 40 | 42 | 44 | 46 | 48 |
| Rest of Europe | 34 | 36 | 38 | 40 | 42 | 44 |
| USA | 6 | 8 | 10 | 12 | 14 | 16 |

### MEN'S SHIRTS

| | | | | | | | |
|---|---|---|---|---|---|---|---|
| UK | 14 | 14.5 | 15 | 15.5 | 16 | 16.5 | 17 |
| Rest of Europe | 36 | 37 | 38 | 39/40 | 41 | 42 | 43 |
| USA | 14 | 14.5 | 15 | 15.5 | 16 | 16.5 | 17 |

### MEN'S SHOES

| | | | | | | |
|---|---|---|---|---|---|---|
| UK | 7 | 7.5 | 8.5 | 9.5 | 10.5 | 11 |
| Rest of Europe | 41 | 42 | 43 | 44 | 45 | 46 |
| USA | 8 | 8.5 | 9.5 | 10.5 | 11.5 | 12 |

### WOMEN'S SHOES

| | | | | | | |
|---|---|---|---|---|---|---|
| UK | 4.5 | 5 | 5.5 | 6 | 6.5 | 7 |
| Rest of Europe | 38 | 38 | 39 | 39 | 40 | 41 |
| USA | 6 | 6.5 | 7 | 7.5 | 8 | 8.5 |

Churches are generally open from 8am–noon and again from 3–6pm. Restaurant hours are generally from noon until 2 or 3pm and from 7pm until 10pm. Museums and attractions are generally closed on Mondays.

## Passports and visas

EU citizens can enter Italy for an unlimited stay with a valid passport. US, Australian, Canadian and New Zealand passport holders must have passports that are valid for at least three months from entry date and can stay anywhere in the EU for up to three months in a six-month period without a prearranged visa.

## Pharmacies

Italian pharmacies (marked *farmacia*, look for the green cross) don't appear to have shelves packed with myriad brands of stock, but are highly competent and helpful in assisting with the minor ailments that beset travellers. For after-hours assistance, ask at your hotel for the nearest open pharmacy – they operate on a roster system.

## Post

Italy's postal system is much maligned and worthy of this reputation. The post office of each city and town is always noted on local maps. Post office opening times vary, but generally they are open Monday to Saturday from 8.30am–7.30pm in major cities. In smaller cities they may close earlier, and in small towns they may shut as early as 1pm, or close for lunch and open again in the afternoon; they may not open at all on Saturdays. Check with your hotel.

## Public holidays

**1 Jan** New Year's Day
**6 Jan** Epiphany
**Mar/Apr** Easter Monday
**25 Apr** Liberation Day
**1 May** Labour Day
**2 June** Anniversary of the Republic
**15 Aug** Feast of the Assumption
**1 Nov** All Saints' Day
**8 Dec** Immaculate Conception
**25 Dec** Christmas Day

## Smoking

Smoking was banned in all but private homes, the open air and specially designated areas as of 2005. *Vietato fumare* (no smoking) signs are generally (albeit grudgingly) adhered to.

## Suggested reading and media

English-language newspapers and periodicals are stocked in larger cities' newsagents and bookstores. Here are some Northern Italian focused titles to whet your appetite for the trip:

*Travelers' Tales Italy: True Stories* by Anne Calcagno (ed), 2001.
*Venice* by Jan Morris, Faber and Faber, 2004.
*A History of Contemporary Italy: Society and Politics, 1943–1988* by Paul Ginsborg, Palgrave Macmillan, 2003.
*The Dark Heart of Italy* by Tobias Jones, North Point Press, 2005.
*A Season with Verona: Travels Around*

*Italy in Search of Illusion, National Character, and…Goals!* by Tim Parks, Arcade Publishing, 2002.

## Tax

Most hotels have a 9 per cent VAT, while top-end hotels have a 12 per cent VAT. Restaurants don't charge a VAT, but will add 10–15 per cent to the bill. If you are buying luxury items to take out of Italy, you may be eligible to receive a tax refund if you are not an EU resident. It's worth looking for shops displaying the Tax Free Shopping logo. For more information visit the Global Refund website (*www.globalrefund.com*).

## Telephones
### Calling home from Italy
**Australia:** *00* + *61* + area code
**Ireland:** *00* + *353* + area code
**New Zealand:** *00* + *64* + area code
**UK:** *00* + *44* + area code
**South Africa:** *00* + *27* + area code
**USA & Canada:** *00* + *1* + area code
**NB:** omit the initial *0* in area codes

### Calling Italy from abroad
Dial the international code *0011* from Australia, *00* from the UK, Ireland and New Zealand, *011* from the USA and Canada, followed by the country code for Italy (*39*) and the number without the first *0* of the area code.

### Public payphones and mobile phones
Public payphones require a *carta telefonica* sold at newsstands. Italy uses the GSM mobile system, and if you are coming from a country that uses that system you might be able to use your phone (check before leaving home). Another option is to purchase a prepaid SIM card in Italy.

To dial a number within Italy always use the area code including the *0*. The area code for Milan is *02*.

## Time
Italy's time zone is Central European (GMT + 1) and has daylight saving from the end of March to the end of September. It is 1 hour ahead of the UK, 6 hours ahead of New York, 1 hour behind South Africa, 10 hours behind Sydney and 12 hours behind Auckland.

## Toilets
Museums, bus and train stations have toilets, and, while a café is a good bet, you will be expected to order to be allowed to use them there. Autogrill stops have toilets that are cleaned regularly. Always carry some tissues as toilet paper is not usually supplied.

## Travellers with disabilities
Cobbled streets, limited parking and a lack of ramps along with seemingly never-ending road and building works do not bode well for travellers with mobility problems. Some hotels have disabled-friendly rooms, and some sights and museums are ramped, but on the whole careful planning is required. Non-profit **Accessible Italy** (*www.accessibleitaly.com*) offers great advice.

# Language

English is quite widely spoken in Northern Italy and those who deal with travellers regularly will generally speak English fluently. While this is good news for visitors, everywhere locals are pleased when you at least begin with *Buon giorno* (Good day).

## PRONUNCIATION

**c and cc** = ch if before e and i, as in 'cheap', otherwise like a k

**ch** = before e and i, is hard, like a k

**g and gg** = soft, like a j, if before e and i, as in 'George'

**gh** = hard, as in 'gorge'

**g** = soft, rolling sound with the g almost silent

**gn** = ny, as in 'canyon'

**gl** = ll, as in 'medallion'

**q** = kw, as in 'quick'

**sc** = soft before an e or an i, as in 'shed'

**sch** = hard, as in 'skip'

**z** = ts except when it starts a word, then ds

## EVERYDAY EXPRESSIONS

| English | Italian |
|---|---|
| Hello | **Ciao** |
| Goodbye | **Arrivederci** |
| Good morning | **Buon giorno** |
| Good afternoon | **Buona sera** |
| Good evening | **Buona sera** |
| Goodnight | **Buona notte** |
| Please | **Per favore** |

| | |
|---|---|
| Thank you | **Grazie** |
| You're welcome | **Prego** |
| I'm sorry | **Mi dispiace** |
| I don't understand | **Non capisco** |
| Excuse me (to get past someone) | **Scusi/Permesso** |
| Yes | **Sì** |
| No | **No** |
| OK | **Va bene** |
| Go away! | **Va via!** |
| Cheers! | **Salute!** |
| At what time... ? | **A che ora... ?** |
| Do you speak English? | **Parla inglese?** |
| I don't speak Italian | **Non parlo italiano** |
| Where is... ? | **Dove... ?** |
| There is/are… | **C'è/Ci sono…** |
| There is/are not… | **Non c'è/Non ci sono…** |
| I want… | **Voglio…** |
| I would like… | **Vorrei…** |
| How much? | **Quanto?** |
| The bill, please | **Il conto, per favore** |
| Big/little | **Grande/piccolo** |
| Hot/cold | **Caldo/freddo** |
| Open/closed | **Aperto/chiuso** |
| Right/left | **Destra/sinistra** |

| | | NUMBERS | |
|---|---|---|---|
| Good/bad | **Buono/cattivo** | 1 | **Uno** |
| Fast/slow | **Presto/lento** | 2 | **Due** |
| Much/little | **Molto/poco** | 3 | **Tre** |
| Expensive/cheap | **Caro/economico** | 4 | **Quattro** |
| Money | **Soldi** | 5 | **Cinque** |
| Toilet | **La toilette/** | 6 | **Sei** |
| | **Il gabinetto** | 7 | **Sette** |
| Men's toilet | **Signori** | 8 | **Otto** |
| Women's toilet | **Signore/Dame** | 9 | **Nove** |
| Today | **Oggi** | 10 | **Dieci** |
| Yesterday | **Ieri** | 11 | **Undici** |
| Tomorrow | **Domani** | 12 | **Dodici** |
| What is the time? | **Che ore sono?** | 13 | **Tredici** |
| | | 14 | **Quattordici** |
| **DAYS OF THE WEEK** | | 15 | **Quindici** |
| Monday | **Lunedì** | 16 | **Sedici** |
| Tuesday | **Martedì** | 17 | **Diciassette** |
| Wednesday | **Mercoledì** | 18 | **Diciotto** |
| Thursday | **Giovedì** | 19 | **Diciannove** |
| Friday | **Venerdì** | 20 | **Venti** |
| Saturday | **Sabato** | 21 | **Ventuno** |
| Sunday | **Domenica** | 22 | **Ventidue** |
| | | 30 | **Trenta** |
| **MONTHS OF THE YEAR** | | 40 | **Quaranta** |
| January | **Gennaio** | 50 | **Cinquanta** |
| February | **Febbraio** | 60 | **Sessanta** |
| March | **Marzo** | 70 | **Settanta** |
| April | **Aprile** | 80 | **Ottanta** |
| May | **Maggio** | 90 | **Novanta** |
| June | **Giugno** | 100 | **Cento** |
| July | **Luglio** | 200 | **Duecento** |
| August | **Agosto** | 500 | **Cinquecento** |
| September | **Settembre** | 1,000 | **Mille** |
| October | **Ottobre** | | |
| November | **Novembre** | | |
| December | **Dicembre** | | |

# Emergencies

## Emergency telephone numbers
Ambulance (*ambulanza*) *118*
Emergencies (*pronto soccorso*) *113*
Fire (*vigili del fuoco*) *115*
Police (*carabinieri*) *112*
Automobile Club d'Italia (ACI)
Breakdown Service *116*

## Medical services
### Casualty
If you need to visit the casualty ward of a hospital always ask for the nearest one that's likely to have the shortest waiting time – your hotel should be able to help you. It's probably a good idea to take along your passport or other ID, just in case. EU visitors should take their EHIC card (*see below*).

### Doctors
If you need non-urgent medical treatment, get a recommendation for an English-speaking doctor (*medico*) from your hotel. If you need dental work, once again ask your hotel for a list of local dentists (*dentiste*). If you wear glasses or use contact lenses and they are lost or damaged, it's best to take a copy of your prescription to save having an optometrist (*ottico*) having to retest your eyes.

### Health and insurance
The most common health concern for visitors to Northern Italy is diarrhoea. The risk of this is reduced by drinking bottled water only, avoiding raw or undercooked seafood or meat and raw fruits that you haven't peeled yourself. Most bouts of diarrhoea pass within a few days.

While your resident country might have emergency medical cover arrangements with Italy, it's always a good idea (and good for peace of mind) to have insurance to cover against theft or loss of luggage as well as illness or injury. Under an EU reciprocal arrangement, visitors from EU countries are entitled to medical treatment, but should obtain a free European Health Insurance Card (EHIC) from *www.ehic.org.uk* or from post offices, or by phoning *0845 606 2030*. This should be presented to the doctor if possible before treatment or a consultation starts. While such arrangements usually take care of emergency medical situations, they do not generally cover dental or optical needs as well.

Note that a general policy might not cover so-called dangerous sports such as kite boarding and skiing.

## Safety and crime
Pickpockets and purse-snatchers are the main concern for visitors to Northern Italy, and places with a high density of tourists, such as Stazione Centrale and Piazza Duomo in Milan, are prime locations for these acts to occur. Expensive cameras are also a target.

Never leave handbags or cameras at your feet when in alfresco restaurants and bars. Car thieves are also a problem in Italy, so be sure to remove all valuables from your car when you leave it, or at least out of sight.

## Lost property

Most railway stations have lost property offices in major cities. In Milan, the municipality runs a city-wide Lost Property Office (Ufficio Oggetti Rinvenuti; *Via Friuli 30; tel: 02 8845 3907; open: Mon–Fri 9am–4pm*).

## Police

Travellers will notice that there are several levels of police in Italy, distinguished by their different uniforms, such as: the Polizia Urbana (city police) who deal with parking infringements and traffic issues; Polizia Stradale (highway police), who will stop you if you're driving on the wrong side of the road; and Carabinieri (military-style police), who deal with more serious crimes.

## Embassies and consulates

### Foreign consulates in Northern Italy
**Australia**
*3rd Floor, Via Borgogna 2, Milan.*
*Tel: 02 777 041.*
**Canada**
*Riviera Ruzzante 25, Padova.*
*Tel: 049 876 4833.*
**Ireland**
*Honorary Consulate:*
*Piazza S. Pietro in Gessate 2, Milan.*
*Tel: 02 5518 7569.*

**New Zealand**
*Via Terraggio, 17, Milan.*
*Tel: 02 721 7001.*
**South Africa**
*Vicolo San Giovanni Sul Muro 4, Milan.*
*Tel: 02 885 8581.*
**UK**
*Via San Paolo 7, Milan. Tel: 02 733 001.*
**USA**
*Via Principe Amadeo 2/10, Milan.*
*Tel: 02 290 351.*

### Italian embassies abroad
**Australia**
*Level 45, 1 Macquarie Place, Sydney,*
*NSW 2000. Tel: (02) 9392 7900 509.*
*12 Grey St, Deakin, ACT 2600.*
*Tel: (02) 6273 3333.*
**Canada**
*275 Slater St, Ottawa, Ontario K1P 5H9.*
*Tel: (613) 232 2401.*
**Ireland**
*63–65 Northumberland Rd, Dublin 4.*
*Tel: (01) 660 1744.*
**New Zealand**
*34 Grant Rd, Thorndon, Wellington.*
*Tel: (04) 499 4186.*
**UK**
*38 Eaton Place, London SW1X 8AN.*
*Tel: (020) 7235 9371.*
*7 Richmond Park, Belfast.*
*Tel: (028) 9066 8854.*
**USA**
*690 Park Ave, New York.*
*Tel: (212) 737 9100 or 439 8600.*
*12400 Wilshire Blvd, Suite 300,*
*Los Angeles. Tel: (310) 820 0622.*
*1601 Fuller St NW, Washington DC.*
*Tel: (202) 328 5500.*

# Directory

## Accommodation price guide

Prices of accommodation are based on a double room per night for two people sharing, with breakfast.

| | |
|---|---|
| ★ | up to €100 |
| ★★ | €100–€140 |
| ★★★ | €140–€220 |
| ★★★★ | over €220 |

## Eating out price guide

Prices are based on an average three-course meal for one, without drinks.

| | |
|---|---|
| ★ | up to €30 |
| ★★ | €30–€60 |
| ★★★ | €60–€100 |
| ★★★★ | over €100 |

Italian restaurants, including *trattorie*, tend to open for lunch from noon until 2.30pm (occasionally 11.30am–3pm). Dinner is usually served from 8pm until 10.30pm, although in tourist areas they may open at 7–7.30pm for foreigners, and stay open later for Italian tourists.

*Enoteche* and *osterie* will sometimes open only in the evenings for drinks and for dinner. Be aware that in small villages some places will close on a whim if there isn't anybody around.

## PIEMONTE & VALLE D'AOSTA

### Alba

**ACCOMMODATION**

**La Meridiana ★**

Overlooking Alba's historic centre, this B&B offers spacious and well-kept rooms and apartments. A good base for exploring the region, with friendly, helpful hosts.
*Località Altavilla.*
*Tel: (0173) 440 112.*

**EATING OUT**

**Osteria dell'Arco ★★**

A 'Slow Food' eatery that takes its wines very seriously. It's one of the homes of traditional local dishes (seasonally available), cooked with care and respect for traditions.
*Piazza Savona 5.*
*Tel: (0173) 363 974.*
*www.osteriadellarco.it*

### Aosta Region

**ACCOMMODATION**

**Bed and Breakfast Aosta ★**

A simple B&B that only has a couple of rooms but enough charm to make it a worthwhile stay while touring the Aosta valley.
*Via E Aubert 50, Aosta.*
*Tel: (0165) 363 006.*
*www.bedbreakfastaosta.it*

**Casa Ospitaliera del Gran San Bernardo ★**

Popular with activity-based visitors (skiers, hikers and climbers) this 12th-century castle is run by an order of monks and is about 15km (9 miles) from Aosta.
*Rue De Flassin 3, Saint-Oyen. Tel: (0165) 78247.*

**EATING OUT**

**Praetoria ★★**

A local favourite for its hearty, good-value

home-made fare and convivial atmosphere, finishing a plate of pasta here warrants a good walk afterwards.
*Via S. Anselmo 9.*
*Tel: (0165) 44356.*

**Vecchio Ristoro ★★★**
One of the most creative and elegant restaurants in the valley, the chef-owner excels in producing modern takes on classic dishes of the region. Exquisite presentation from start to finish.
*Via Tourneuve 4.*
*Tel: (0165) 33238.*

**Giardino Botanico Alpino Saussurea**
A hike through these sub-Alpine gardens is a must for lovers of wild flowers. Deciduous shrubs such as the avalanche-resistant green alder, edible blueberries, and the dwarfed juniper all make appearances.
*Pavillon du Mont Fréty, Courmayeur (first station on the Monte Bianco cable car).*
*Tel: (0333) 446 29 59.*
*www.saussurea.net. Open: Jun–Sept 9am–5pm. Admission charge.*

**Osservatorio Astronomico della Regione Autonoma Valle d'Aosta**
The excellent astronomical observatory hosts a range of activities and programmes for the general public, especially children.
*Lignan 39, Saint-Barthélemy.*
*Tel: (0165) 770 050.*
*www.oavda.it. Open: Apr–Sept daytime from 4.30pm, night-time from 9.30pm; Oct–Mar daytime from 3pm, night-time from 9pm. Pre-booked visits only.*

**Le Passeggiate Nel Cielo, Pila**
The 'Promenade in the Sky' is a series of superb signposted walking trails that climb and cross the mountain tops. They are outlined in an excellent brochure with a map, trail names, duration and level of fitness required. The map is available from local tourist offices or see *www.pila.it*, *www.pilaturismo.it* or *www.comune.gressan.ao.it*

**Rafting Adventure**
This reputable organisation offers a range of rafting

experiences from group excursions to weekend-long adventures.
*Frazione Perolle, Châtillon.*
*Tel: (0166) 563 289. www. raftingadventure.com*

**Thermes (Spas)**
The Valle d'Aosta area is home to a huge number of thermal mountain spas offering various therapies and treatments. Notable spas include **Institut Hydrothermal de Lurisia** (*www.lurisia.it*), **Institut Thermal de Vinadio** (*www. thermedivinadio.com*), **Thermes Royaux de Valdieri** (*www. termevaldierei.it*) and **Thermes d'Acqui** (*www. termediacqui.it*). Local tourist offices have more information on spas.

## Asti
**Albergo Castiglione ★★**
Located right in the heart of a DOCG wine region, this hotel has tastefully designed rooms, a spa and a pool centre.
*Via Cavour 5, Castiglione Tinella.*
*Tel: (0141) 855 410.*
*www.albergocastiglione. com*

**Relais San Maurizio** ★★★
A 17th-century monastery is the home of this considerably grand hotel. Beautiful rooms with all modern amenities and a superb Michelin-starred cellar restaurant.
*Località San Maurizio 39, Santo Stefano Belbo.*
*Tel: (0141) 841 900.*
*www.relaissanmaurizio.it*

**EATING OUT**
**L'Angolo del Beato** ★★★
This intimate, almost homely restaurant is the epitome of the epicurean ethos of the region – local seasonal ingredients cooked with care and served with matching great local wines.
*Via Guttuari 12.*
*Tel: (0141) 531 668.*
*www.angolodelbeato.it*

**Barolo**
**EATING OUT**
**La Cantinetta** ★★★
Run by two enthusiastic brothers, the cuisine here runs from traditional regional classics to exciting, innovative dishes.
*Via Roma 33.*
*Tel: (0173) 56198.*

**ENTERTAINMENT**
**Enoteca Regionale del Barolo**
The wine promotion office has a showroom and offers the chance of tasting great regional wines at reasonable prices.
*Castello Falletti.*
*Tel: (0173) 56277.*
*www.baroloworld.it.*
*Open: Mar–Oct Fri–Wed 10am–12.30pm & 3–6pm; Nov–Dec & Feb 10am–4.30pm. Closed: Jan.*

**Turin**
**ACCOMMODATION**
**Hotel Victoria** ★★
A longtime favourite for its family atmosphere, it belies its large number of rooms with personal service. The furnishings sometimes border on chintzy, but the breakfast room and spa really are worth it.
*Via Nino Costa 4.*
*Tel: (011) 561 19 09. www.hotelvictoria-torino.com*
**Orso Poeta** ★★
A charming B&B with only two rooms, it's worth trying to secure one for the taste of real Turin life. Set in a 19th-century historic building, one of the rooms has a

terrace – both have wonderful views.
*Corso Vittorio Emanuele II 10.*
*Tel: (011) 517 89 96.*
*www.orsopoeta-bed-and-breakfast.it*
**Art+Tech** ★★★★
This Meridien property, designed by renowned architect Renzo Piano, is a stylish refurbishment of a former Fiat factory.
*Via Nizza 230.*
*Tel: (011) 664 20 00.*
*www.starwoodhotels.com*
**Golden Palace** ★★★★
Located in the historic centre, the austere exterior turns to warmth inside this five-star hotel that opened prior to the 2006 Winter Olympics – the use of gold, silver and bronze colours is no accident. Excellent service.
*Via dell'Arcivescovado 18.*
*Tel: (011) 551 21 11.*
*www.thi-hotels.com*

**EATING OUT**
**Locanda di Betty** ★
A smart choice for a city-centre lunch, it serves honest local fare and generous pastas, with an especially good *ragù*. There are only a few outdoor tables.

*Via Conte Giambattista Bogino 17.*
*Tel: (011) 817 05 83.*

**Marechiaro** ★
Excellent food and friendly service. The *bresaola* and *carpaccio* make for great starters and the pastas are especially good.
*Via San Francesco d'Assisi 21.*
*Tel: (011) 535 757. www. marechiaroristorante.it*

**Taverna dell Rose** ★★
This venerable eatery with its farmhouse atmosphere keeps locals and visitors coming back for its simple, honest fare. Great *antipasto* plates, fine risottos and plenty of tables sharing big slabs of beef.
*Via Massena 24.*
*Tel: (011) 538 345.*

**Ristorante del Cambio** ★★★
The city's most elegant and romantic restaurant has been in operation since 1859 and it's still a hot table for foodies coming to Turin. An unapologetically old-fashioned menu features dishes such as beef cheek in Barolo served with polenta.

*Piazza Carignano 2.*
*Tel: (011) 546 690.*

## ENTERTAINMENT
### Cafés
Turin is famous for its old-style elegant cafés. **Caffè Mulafsano** (*Piazza Castello 15*) is a small, graceful café; **Al Bicerin** (*Piazza della Consolata 5*) dates from 1763 while **San Tommaso 10** (*Via San Tommaso 10*) puts a new face on the original Lavazza coffee store.

### Church concerts
The cathedrals and churches of Northern Italian cities and towns are the venues for regular performances by chamber orchestras, pianists and choirs. You will typically see posters plastered around towns in the days leading up to the events and leaflets handed out in squares (especially in Venice). You can also get information from tourist offices or your hotel.

### Docks Dora
These renovated warehouses contain bars, cafés, clubs, live music

venues and alternative theatres. Locals rarely arrive at cafés and bars before 10pm or at clubs before midnight.
*Via Valprato 68.*
*Tel: (011) 280 251.*

**Teatro Regio**
Turin's opera house is one of Italy's best, and, while opening nights sell out well in advance, it's generally possible to get tickets for performances from the box office on the same day.
*Piazza Castello. Tel: (011) 881 5241/881 5557.*
*www.teatroregio.torino.it*

## SPORT AND LEISURE
**Turin Po River Park**
This riverside conservation area covers 40,000ha (99,000 acres) across three provinces and takes in myriad nature reserves with an immense range of flora and birdlife. There are botanical gardens, walking and cycling tracks, equestrian clubs, canoeing, kayaking and rowing opportunities, and picnic facilities. Local tourist offices will have details. Also see *www.turismotorino.org*

## LIGURIA
### Camogli
#### ACCOMMODATION
**Villa Rosmarino ★★★**
Charming and stylish
B&B overlooking
Camogli. Exquisitely
restored, this small
'palace' dates to 1907.
Wonderful hosts.
*Via Figari 38.*
*Tel: (0185) 771 580.*
*www.villarosmarino.com*

#### EATING OUT
**La Cucina de Nonna
Nina ★★**
Outside of Camogli, this
restaurant is upstairs in
a classic local home.
Home-made pasta and
fish bought directly from
local fishermen are key to
the menu.
*Via Molfino 126, San
Rocco di Camogli.*
*Tel: (0185) 773 835.*
*www.nonnanina.it*
**Ristorante da Paolo ★★**
Tucked away up a side
street, the location
leaves this restaurant
almost immune to the
passing traffic, but not
to food lovers who
come for the fresh
seafood.
*Via S. Fortunato 14.*
*Tel: (0185) 773 595.*

#### SPORT AND LEISURE
**Golfo Paradise
(Paradise Gulf)**
This company offers
frequent boat services
between Camogli,
Portofino, the Cinque
Terre villages and
Portovenere.
*Via Scalo 2.*
*Tel: (0185) 772 091.*
*www.golfoparadiso.it*

### Cinque Terre
#### ACCOMMODATION
**L'Antica Terrazza ★**
This renovated pension
has only four rooms, each
with en suite. They have
satellite TV and a/c, and
views over an enchanting
square in the town.
*Vicolo San Martino 1,
Monterosso.*
*Tel: (0187) 817 499.*
**Ca' d'Andrean ★**
A small, simple hotel, this
is a good option in one of
the quieter places. Some
rooms have balconies.
*Via Discovolo 101,
Manarola.*
*Tel: (0187) 920 040.*

#### EATING OUT
**Gambero Rosso ★★**
A highly regarded
*trattoria*, it turns out
mouthwatering plates of
seafood with pasta and
delicious risotto.
*Piazza Marconi 7,
Vernazza.*
*Tel: (0187) 812 265.*
**Ripa del Sole ★★**
A decent restaurant
with a delightful summer
terrace, the specialities
of the house are seafood,
fresh pasta and fine
local wines.
*Via de' Gaspari 282,
Riomaggiore.*
*Tel: (0187) 920 143.*
**Il Gigante ★★★**
This popular *trattoria* is
a little more upmarket
than many. They do
wonderful seafood dishes.
*Via IV Novembre 9,
Monterosso.*
*Tel: (0187) 817401.*
*Reservations essential.*

#### SPORT AND LEISURE
**Walking the Cinque
Terre**
The classic walk of the
'five lands' can be done
in one day, if you so
wish. Trail number two
is the walk most people
take (starting at
Riomaggiore), passing all
five villages and covering
around 13km (8 miles).
There are frequent
local trains between all

five villages. Tickets can be bought from the station in each village. The Cinque Terre Card offers unlimited travel, as well as access to the national park. There are passes for one, three or seven days, and they are available from train stations and tourist information offices.

## Genova
### ACCOMMODATION
### Bentley Hotel ★★★
A stylish new hotel in the former headquarters of an iron and steel manufacturer, this is Genova's only five-star property. The extensive amenities are perfect for business and leisure guests.
*Via Corsica 4.*
*Tel: (010) 531 51 11.*
*www.thi-hotels.com*
### Bristol Palace ★★★
Once the best place in town, today the hotel is an elegant old pile with plenty of curios and old-school charm. Great location and service.
*Via XX Settembre 35.*
*Tel: (010) 592 541.*
*www.hotelbristolpalace.it*

### Locanda di Palazzo Cicala ★★★
A boutique hotel on the first floor of a 16th-century charmer, this hotel mixes the heritage of the building with contemporary touches.
*Piazza San Lorenzo 16.*
*Tel: (010) 251 88 24.*
*www.palazzocicala.it*

### EATING OUT
### Hostaria Da Cesira ★★
A great, honest little restaurant with a short and sweet menu. Simple dishes such as *trenette al pesto* and tagliatelli with scampi display Italian simplicity at its best.
*Salita Viale Salvatore 19r.*
*Tel: (010) 570 45 59.*
### Maxelâ ★★
For meat lovers, this is heaven. With a counter stocked with great cuts of beef and a slicing machine desperately trying to keep up with orders of *misto crudo* (cold cuts), settle in and take in some serious protein.
*Vico Inferiore del Ferro 9.*
*Tel: (010) 247 4209.*
*www.maxela.it*
### I Tre Merli ★★
This atmospheric old osteria has been

transformed into a great 'cantina' with modernised takes on Genovese classics. It has a wonderful wine list.
*Vico Dietro il Coro Maddalena 26r.*
*Tel: (010) 247 40 95.*
*www.itremerli.it*

## Portofino
### ACCOMMODATION
### Hotel Eden ★★★
A simple but pleasant three-star hotel with a lovely small garden, just a short walk from the harbour.
*Via Dritto 18.*
*Tel: (0185) 269 091. www. hoteledenportofino.com*

### EATING OUT
### Pizzeria El Portico ★
This eatery up from the harbour is the best value in town and serves great pizzas and pastas.
*Via Roma 21.*
*Tel: (0185) 269 239.*

## Portovenere
### EATING OUT
### La Marina da Antonio ★★
The pick of the waterfront restaurants for its friendly service and excellent seafood

dishes such as *Antipasti Misti di Mare* (seafood *antipasti*).
*Piazza Marina 6.*
*Tel: (0187) 790 686.*

## Rapallo
### ACCOMMODATION
**Excelsior Palace Hotel ★★★**
A wonderful, grand old hotel dating from the early 20th century, it's the only five-star hotel along this stretch of coast. It's worth taking a spacious deluxe room with breathtaking views.
*Via San Michele di Pagana 8.*
*Tel: (0185) 230 666.*
*www.thi-hotels.com*

### EATING OUT
**Trattoria di Mario ★★**
This *trattoria* is a long-time favourite, known for its seafood pastas and grilled fish.
*Piazza Garibaldi 23.*
*Tel: (0185) 51736.*

## Sanremo
### ACCOMMODATION
**Hotel Royal ★★★★**
A classic old pile on the Riviera, it's a massive hotel with an enormous swimming pool in a subtropical garden.
*Corso Imperatrice 80.*
*Tel: (0184) 5391. www. royalhotelsanremo.com*

### EATING OUT
**Il Sommergibile ★★★**
With a name that translates to 'submarine', you can bet that seafood is the focus of this restaurant – lobster is a speciality.
*Piazza Bresca 12.*
*Tel: (0184) 501 944.*

## EMILIA ROMAGNA
## Bologna
### ACCOMMODATION
**Break 28 B&Bs ★**
Great position and great views from this modest B&B.
*Via Marconi 28.*
*Tel: 333 331 35 60.*

**Hotel Royal Carlton ★★★**
A comfortable hotel with all modern conveniences. It is a short walk to all the main sights.
*Via Montebello 8.*
*Tel: (051) 249361.*
*www.monrifhotels.it*

### EATING OUT
**Diana ★★★**
A local institution since 1920, Diana is an inviting, old-fashioned eatery with formal waiters and a touch of Parisian bistro. Order old Bolognese specials and game and truffles.
*Via Indipendenza 24.*
*Tel: (051) 228 162.*

**Franco Rossi ★★★**
An intimate little restaurant with a touch of flamboyance.
*Via Giotto 3.*
*Tel: (051) 238 818.*

### ENTERTAINMENT
**Teatro Comunale**
This splendid 18th-century theatre is the venue for concerts by orchestras and other classical music recitals.
*Largo Respighi 1.*
*Tel: (199) 107 070.*
*www.comunalebologna.it*

## Ferrara
### ACCOMMODATION
**Hotel Ripagrande ★★★**
A former 15th-century palace, the public areas of this hotel are stunning. The rooms are more restrained, but comfortable and with excellent service.
*Via Ripagrande 21.*
*Tel: (0532) 765 250.*
*www.ripagrandehotel.it*

## EATING OUT

**Il Don Giovanni ★★★**
A delightfully intimate
restaurant, its large
vegetable garden is
testament to its belief in
seasonal produce, and
the beautifully presented
plates to the skill in the
kitchen. They have a
wine bar as well.
*Corso Ercole I D'este 1.*
*Tel: (0532) 243 363.*
*www.ildongiovanni.com*

## Modena

### ACCOMMODATION

**Hotel Canalgrande ★★★**
Modena has surprisingly
few good hotels, but the
faded grandeur of this
one wins guests over.
Lovely gardens and a
short walk to the sights.
*Corso Canalgrande 6.*
*Tel: (059) 217 160.*
*www.canalgrandehotel.it*

### EATING OUT

**Da Enzo ★★**
This venerable *trattoria*
serves local specialities
and familiar favourites.
*Via Coltellini 17.*
*Tel: (059) 225 177*

**Hosteria Giusti ★★★**
A classic old restaurant
suitably adjacent to one
of the world's oldest delis.

Everything is made on the
premises or sourced from
next door.
*Vicolo Squallore 46.*
*Tel: (059) 222 533.*
*www.giusti1605.com*

## Parma

### ACCOMMODATION

**Hotel Verdi ★★**
A handsome hotel with
20 rooms decorated in
Art Nouveau style. The
hotel has a well-regarded
restaurant.
*Via Pasini 18.*
*Tel: (0521) 293 539.*
*www.hotelverdi.it*

**Starhotels du Parc ★★★**
A Liberty-style hotel
located in a renovated
old ice factory, close to
the historic centre.
*Viale Piacenza 12c.*
*Tel: (0521) 292 929.*
*www.starhotels.it*

### EATING OUT

**Angiol d'Or ★★**
Tucked away in a corner
of Piazza del Duomo,
this modern restaurant
is as popular with locals
as it is with visitors.
Great-quality meats.
*Vicolo Scutellari 1.*
*Tel: (0521) 282 632.*

**Gallo d'Oro ★★**
A classic, simple

restaurant, it's known
for its fantastic meat
*antipasti*, tortelli
pasta and excellent
Parmigiano cheese.
*Via Borgo della Salina 3.*
*Tel: (0521) 208 846.*
*www.gallodororistorante.it*

**Al Tramezzo ★★**
The simple décor of
Al Tramezzo belies its
reputation as one of the
best restaurants in the
region. The aged hams
are legendary.
*Via Alberto Del Bono 5b.*
*Tel: (0521) 487 906.*
*www.altramezzo.it*

**Trattoria del
Tribunale ★★**
This popular eatery fills
a massive terrace in the
warmer months where
endless plates of fantastic
*prosciutto di Parma* (some
of the town's best) are
run out to hungry diners.
It's a great place to try
specials such as the *trippa
alla parmigiana* (tripe).
*Vicolo Politi 5.*
*Tel: (0521) 285 527. www.
trattoriadeltribunale.it*

### ENTERTAINMENT

**Teatro Regio**
Parma's premier opera,
music and theatre venue.
*Via Garibaldi 16.*

Tel: (0521) 218 678/
039 399.
www.teatroregioparma.
torino.org

### Ravenna

**ACCOMMODATION**

**Albergo Cappello ★★★**

Simply the best place in
town, this 14th-century
palace has only seven
uniquely decorated
rooms, all with plenty of
personality. Great
restaurant and wine bar.
Via IV Novembre 41.
Tel: (0544) 219 813.
www.albergocappello.it

**EATING OUT**

**Ristorante Bella
Venezia ★★**

A favourite with locals,
this family-run restaurant
serves fantastic regional
specials. The pasta is
handmade and served
with seasonal ingredients.
Via 4 Novembre 16.
Tel: (0544) 212 746.
www.bellavenezia.it

## LOMBARDIA

### Bergamo

**ACCOMMODATION**

**Bed & Breakfast
Bergamo ★–★★**

This Bed and Breakfast
Association has an array
of excellent B&Bs in
Bergamo on its books.
Various locations.
www.bedandbergamo.it

**Hotel Piazza Vecchia ★★**

This small hotel offers
lovely rooms just a few
metres from the best
restaurants in town.
Via Colleoni 3.
Tel: (035) 428 42 11.
www.hotelpiazzavecchia.it

**EATING OUT**

**Colleoni &
Dell'Angelo ★★**

An elegant restaurant
serving modern takes on
local favourite dishes.
Casoncelli, Bergamo's
typical ravioli, with sage,
butter and Parmesan,
is a must. Interesting
wine list and attentive
service.
Piazza Vecchia 7.
Tel: (035) 232 596. www.
colleonidellangelo.com

**Al Donizetti ★★**

It is hard to miss this
great casual eatery
during the warmer
months as the outdoor
arcade is packed full
of patrons. Excellent
polenta dishes.
Via Combito 17a.
Tel: (035) 242 661.
www.donizetti.it

**Vineria Cozzi ★★**

A great casual wine bar
with marble-topped
tables, locals know the
food here is just as good
as the wine list. Great
polenta dishes, and their
pasta with duck
Bolognese is divine.
Via B. Colleoni 22.
Tel: (035) 238 836.
www.vineriacozzi.it

**SPORT AND LEISURE**

**Guided tours**

The excellent Bergamo
tourist offices offer a
number of guided tours,
including informative
itineraries in the old city
and tours along trails in
the Bergamo hills.
Via Gombito 13.
Tel: (035) 242 226.

### Cremona

**ACCOMMODATION**

**Dellearti Design
Hotel ★★★**

This 'design' hotel's
industrial theme is
showing its age a little,
but it's hard to find fault
with the location, one
street away from the
main square.
Via Bonomelli 8.
Tel: (0372) 23131.
www.dellearti.com

EATING OUT

**La Sosta ★★**

A centrally located local favourite, the home-made salami and gnocchi are the order of the day in this old wood-panelled restaurant.
*Via Vescovo Sicardo 9. Tel: (0372) 456 656.*

## Lago di Como

ACCOMMODATION

**Albergo Terminus ★★★**

This 19th-century, Liberty-style hotel has been wonderfully restored and has a splendid location right on the shores of the lake.
*Lungo Lario Trieste 14, Como. Tel: (031) 329 111. www.albergoterminus.com*

**Grand Hotel Tremezzo ★★★★**

This delightful 1910 hotel is adjacent to Villa Carlotta. The swimming pool ingeniously located on the lake is a hit with children.
*Via Regina 8, Tremezzo. Tel: (0344) 42491. www. grandhoteltremezzo.com*

**Grand Hotel Villa Serbelloni ★★★★**

One of the oldest and arguably the grandest hotel of the area. A large pool, two restaurants (one with views and one with a Michelin Star) and lovely gardens. Book a room with a view.
*Via Roma 1, Bellagio. Tel: (031) 950 216. www.villaserbelloni.com*

EATING OUT

**Il Carrettiere ★**

While it might appear odd to be dining at a homely Sicilian-focused restaurant here in Como, Il Carrettiere serves some of the heartiest food in town. Tasty pizzas, great seafood risotto and some of the best mixed seafood (*fritto misto*) around.
*Via Coloniola 18, Como. Tel: (031) 303 478.*

**L'Antica Riva ★★**

A trip to Como is incomplete without a lakeside seafood feast, and this restaurant fulfils that promise. Try the smoked red tuna carpaccio with fennel, or just order the *Gran antipasto di mare all'Antica Riva*, for a great plate of light seafood.
*Via Lungo Lario Trieste 50, Como. Tel: (031) 305 221. www.anticariva.it*

**Il Gatto Nero ★★**

'The Black Cat' is known for its spectacular views – both of the lake and visiting VIPs. The food is fine, but the romantic setting wins the night.
*Via Monte Santo 69, Rovenna.*
*Tel: (031) 512 042.*

**Hotel Villa Serbelloni ★★★**

This grand hotel has two outstanding restaurants, both under the watchful eye of chef Ettore Bocchia. Foodies will be heading to Mistral, the hotel's creative Michelin-starred restaurant, while the hotel restaurant in a beautiful glass observatory is also notable for its cuisine and service.
*Via Roma 1, Bellagio. Tel: (031) 950 216. www.villaserbelloni.com*

**Vecchia Varenna ★★★**

Being a very short stone's throw from the water on Lake Como means two things – fresh seafood and wonderful views. Vecchia Varenna has both.
*Contrada Scoscesa 10, Varenna.*
*Tel: (0341) 830793.*

### Sport and leisure
### Lake excursions

The organisation governing all water activities on the three main lakes, *Gestione Governativa Navigazione Laghi Maggiore, di Garda e di Como*, in addition to managing all public ferry and boat services around the lakes, offers a range of excursions and themed cruises, including lunch and dinner cruises.
*Via per Cernobbio 18, Como. Tel: (031) 579 211. www.navigazionelaghi.it*

### Rent A Boat

From several points on Lake Como you can rent easy-to-drive speed boats, along with water skis, wake boards and wet suits, from 1 hour to 3 days. Prices start from €75 per hour and go up to €2,250 for 6 days for a glamorous Sessa S26.
*Tel: (0380) 843 5253. www.rentland.it*

### Seaplane tours

Seaplanes have been flying on Lake Como since 1913, and one of the most popular activities to do on the lake is to take a scenic flight. This

organisation has been established since 1930 and has a solid reputation.
*Aero Club Como, Viale Masia 44, Como. Tel: (031) 574 495. www.aeroclubcomo.com*

## Lago di Garda
### Accommodation
### Locanda Agli Angeli ★★

This friendly, family-run hotel and restaurant is a gem. The rooms vary in size (and rates) but all are warm and inviting.
*Piazza Garibaldi 2, Gardone Riviera. Tel: (0365) 20832. www.agliangeli.com*

### Gran Hotel Gardone ★★★★

The grand old dame of the Gardone Riviera is a little worn around the edges but still endearingly majestic. The lake is literally right outside your window.
*Via Zanardelli 84, Gardone Riviera. Tel: (0365) 20261. www.grangardone.it*

### Hotel Sirmione ★★★★

This hotel has an enviable position adjacent to the castle, and despite the summer crowds that fill the

nearby characterful streets, the hotel is a lovely retreat – especially with the wonderful spa.
*Piazza Castello 19, Sirmione. Tel: (030) 916 192. www.termedisirmione.com*

### Eating out
### Agli Angeli ★★

Excellent, often-inventive seasonal dishes from the kitchen. Book an outside table in warmer months.
*Piazza Garibaldi 2, Gardone Riviera. Tel: (0365) 20832. www.agliangeli.com*

### La Rucola ★★★★

This elegant, Michelin-starred establishment has three dining rooms that provide a great setting for creative, finely tuned and often whimsical cuisine. Excellent wines.
*Via Strentelle 3, Sirmione. Tel: (030) 916 326. www.ristorantelarucola.it*

### Villa Fiordaliso ★★★★

The Liberty-style former home of Mussolini's mistress serves wonderfully crafted, seafood-focused cuisine that is as beautiful to

look at as it is to eat.
*Via Zanardelli 150,
Gardone Riviera.
Tel: (0365) 20158.
www.villafiordaliso.it*

### SPORT AND LEISURE

**Aquaria**

This thermal spa offers swimming pools, whirlpools and a range of spa treatments.
*Piazza Don A Piatti 1,
Centro Storico di
Sirmione.
Tel: (030) 916 044.
www.termedisirmione.com*

**CitySightseeing Garda**

This is a popular hop-on hop-off bus tour with tickets valid for 24 hours and audio-guide commentaries available in different languages. It does a continuous circuit of the southern part of Lake Garda and stops at most of its theme parks.
*www.garda.city-sightseeing.it*

**Guided tours**

The Sirmione ProLoco tourist office has teamed up with the local Hotels and Restaurants Association to offer a number of guided tours in Sirmione and around

Lake Garda, from tours to historic sites to 'A Glass of History' Wine Tour which visits the best wineries in the area.
*Tel: (030) 919 322. www.comune.sirmione.bs.it*

**Theme parks**

Lake Garda is home to a number of family-oriented theme parks including a Disneyland-like **Gardaland** (*www.gardaland.it*), **Movieland** (*www.movieland.it*), **Medieval Times** (*www.medievaltimes.it*), **Sea Life Aquarium** (*www.seaeurope.com*), **AquaParadise** (*www.aquaparadise.it*), **Il Parco Acquatico Cavour** (*www.parcoacquaticocavour.it*), **Jungle Adventure** (*www.jungleadventure.it*), and an animal safari park called **Parco Natura Viva** (*www.parconaturaviva.it*).

## Lago Maggiore

### ACCOMMODATION

**Il Sole di Ranco** ★★★

This small inn is a foodies' destination as well as a hotel. Accommodation is in two villas on the lake.
*Piazza Venezia 5, Ranco.
Tel: (0331) 976 507.
www.ilsolediranco.it*

**Grand Hotel des Îles Borromées** ★★★★

This five-star luxury property is a stunner, built in 1861. The opulent rooms, the vast public areas and two outdoor heated swimming pools encourage relaxing.
*Corso Umberto I 67, Stresa.
Tel: (0323) 938 938.
www.borromees.it*

### EATING OUT

**Da Cesare** ★★

This restaurant has outdoor tables and a fine menu of local specialities.
*Via Mazzini 14, Verbania.
Tel: (0323) 31386.*

**Il Sole di Ranco** ★★★

This family-run restaurant has an enviable reputation, and chef Davide Brovelli's creative cuisine keeps this well and truly alive. Expect superbly cooked lake fish and seasonal vegetables.
*Piazza Venezia 5, Ranco.
Tel: (0331) 97 65 07.
www.ilsolediranco.it*

## Lago d'Orta

### ACCOMMODATION

**Villa Crespi** ★★★★

Villa Crespi is certainly Northern Italy's most

original hotel, having been built in a Moorish style (complete with an ornate minaret) in 1879 by Cristoforo Benigno Crespi, a cotton trader besotted with Baghdad. The wildly creative Italian cuisine of the restaurant is something else.

*Via G. Fava 18, Orta San Giulio.*
*Tel: (0322) 911 902.*
*www.hotelvillacrespi.it*

### EATING OUT
**Salera 16 ★**
This contemporary café opposite the waterfront has a great-value menu of the day with simple pastas and salads. The terrace gets crowded with locals in summer.
*Piazza Salera 16, Omegna.*
*Tel: 349 215 16 32 (mobile).*
**Villa Crespi ★★★★**
Acclaimed chef Antonino Cannavacciuolo appears far too young to have a Michelin star, let alone two, but his thoughtful, often whimsical dishes show beautiful balance and an intelligent approach to using prime local ingredients.

*Via G. Fava 18,*
*Orta San Giulio.*
*Tel: (0322) 911 902.*
*www.hotelvillacrespi.it*

### SPORT AND LEISURE
**Giro Lago**
The Giro Lago consists of over 500km (310 miles) of itineraries you can do on bike and on foot, including two scenic circuits of the lake.
*Ecomuseo del Lago d'Orta e Mottarone. Piazza Unita d'Italia 2, Pettenasco.*
*Tel: (0323) 89622.*
*www.lagodorta.net*

## Mantova
### ACCOMMODATION
**Hotel San Lorenzo ★★★**
An elegant hotel with spacious rooms and 19th-century furnishings. There's a wonderful rooftop terrace where you can have breakfast.
*Piazza Concordia 14.*
*Tel: (0376) 220 500.*
*www.hotelsanlorenzo.it*

### EATING OUT
**Ambasciata ★★★★**
In an elegant, if a little off-beat restaurant, the creations from Romano Tamani are robust, flavourful and more fun

than you'd expect from such a high-profile restaurant.
*Via Martiri di Belfiore 33, Quistello.*
*Tel: (0376) 619 169.*

## Milan
### ACCOMMODATION
**Antica Locanda dei Mercanti ★★**
This former residential palazzo has been turned into a cosy hotel. Rooms with a terrace are the most romantic.
*Via San Tomaso 8.*
*Tel: (02) 805 40 80.*
*www.locanda.it*
**Antica Locanda Solferino ★★**
A fashionista's favourite, at times this hotel feels like more of a private club. Rooms are delightfully and uniquely decorated with Art Nouveau or late 19th-century pieces.
*Via Castelfidardo 2.*
*Tel: (02) 657 01 29. www. anticalocandasolferino.it*
**Ariston ★★**
Modern, comfortable three-star hotel with well-appointed rooms and a good position for shopping and nightlife.
*Largo Carrobbio 2.*

*Tel: (02) 7200 0556.*
*www.aristonhotel.com*
**Hotel Vecchia Milano ★★**
This hotel has a good
location. The rooms are
small, but very well kept.
*Via Borromei 4.*
*Tel: (02) 875 042.*
**Park Hyatt Milano ★★★★**
You can't beat the location
of this luxurious hotel –
you literally step outside
the door into Galleria
Vittorio Emanuele II for
some shopping. The
service is exemplary and
the rooms vary in size, but
never in quality.
*Via Tommaso Grossi 1.*
*Tel: (02) 8821 1234. www.*
*milan.park.hyatt.com*
**Sheraton Diana
Majestic ★★★★**
This historic hotel has
never really fallen out of
favour – probably
because most of the
fashion industry ends up
here at some stage during
the fashion weeks.
*Viale Piave 42.*
*Tel: (02) 20581.*
*www.starwoodhotels.com*

**EATING OUT**
**Gnocco Fritto ★**
Not really on the tourist
trail, groups of locals go
here for *gnocco fritto*

(puffy fried dough)
served alongside mouth-
watering plates of
*antipasti*. Great fun.
*Via Pasquale Paoli 2.*
*Tel: (02) 5810 0216.*
**El Brellin ★★**
This long-term favourite
is a good place to try
some local specialities
such as *ossobucco con
risotto Milanese.* Outdoor
seating out the back and
aperitifs out the front.
*Vicolo Dei Lavandai.*
*Tel: (02) 5810 1351.*
**Fabbrica ★★**
Relaxed and casual, with
a short wine list, good
beer and wonderful, fresh
pizzas cooked in wood-
fired ovens.
*Via Alzaia Naviglio
Grande 70.*
*Tel: (02) 835 82 97.*
**Trattoria Bagutta ★★**
This famous *trattoria*
dating from the 1920s is
still wildly popular –
their *antipasti* plates are
legendary.
*Via Bagutta 14–16.*
*Tel: (02) 7600 2767.*
**Le Vigne ★★**
A great little rustic
osteria with a short food
menu and a long wine
list. Shows great touch
with staples such as *fiori*

*di zucca* (stuffed zucchini
flowers) and pastas.
*Ripa di Porta Ticinese 61.*
*Tel: (02) 837 56 17.*
**Joia ★★★**
Milan's vegetarians
rejoice with Joia. A
vegetarian restaurant that
has a Michelin star is no
mean feat, but chef
Pietro Leemann is a chef
with surprising abilities.
*Via Panfilo Castaldi 18.*
*Tel: (02) 2952 2124.*
**Ristorante Cracco ★★★★**
Carlo Cracco's restaurant
is regarded as one of
the world's best and is a
gastronomic temple for
foodies in the heart of
Milan. Cracco updates
Northern Italian dishes
with real inventiveness.
*Via Victor Hugo 4.*
*Tel: (02) 876 774.*

**ENTERTAINMENT**
**Navigli**
*Aperitivo* hour is lively
here, with plenty of bars
to choose from. Luca &
Andrea, and MAG Café
(which has jazz some
nights), both on Alzaia
Naviglio Grande, are
favourites.
**Teatro Alla Scala**
The main booking office
to get tickets for an opera

or music performance at this wonderful theatre is underneath the Duomo. There are last-minute tickets available at the window at the Opera.
*Via Filodrammatici 2.*
*Tel: (02) 7200 3744 (bookings).*
*www.teatroallascala.org*

## VENETO AND FRIULI-VENEZIA GIULIA
### Asolo
#### ACCOMMODATION
**Villa Cipriani ★★★**
A delightful property that feels like a country estate. Lovely rooms, garden views.
*Via Canova 298.*
*Tel: (0423) 523 411.*

#### EATING OUT
**Al Bacaro ★**
This osteria serves up hearty fare to a mainly local crowd. There is a casual section and a more 'formal' one.
*Via Browning 165.*
*Tel: (0423) 55150.*
**Restaurant Villa Cipriani ★★**
It's worth trying to get to this restaurant before dark – the views are quite stunning. The regional food matches

the views and the service is exemplary.
*Via Canova 298.*
*Tel: (0423) 523 411.*

### Treviso
#### ACCOMMODATION
**Carlton Hotel ★★**
Good clean hotel that's in a bit of a time-warp but has great views of the town.
*Largo di Porta Altinia 15.*
*Tel: (0422) 411 611.*
*www.hotelcarlton.it*

#### EATING OUT
**Beccherie ★★**
While most people come for the meat and risotto dishes this restaurant harbours a secret – *tiramisu*, the famous Italian dessert, is claimed to have been invented here by pastry chef Roberto Linguanotto.
*Piazza Ancilotto.*
*Tel: (0422) 540 871.*

### Trieste
#### ACCOMMODATION
**Urban Hotel Design ★★★**
A surprisingly hip, minimalist hotel for grand old Trieste, it's a breath of fresh air in a city that doesn't have great sleeping options.

Good location.
*Androna Chiusa 4.*
*Tel: (040) 302 065.*
*www.urbanhotel.it*

#### EATING OUT
**Al Ritrovo Marittimo ★★**
A great casual eatery serving up plenty of seafood specials. The *fritto misto* (fried mixed seafood) is one of the best.
*Via del Lazzaretto Vecchio 3.*
*Tel: (040) 301 377.*

### Venice
#### ACCOMMODATION
**3749 Ponte Chiodo ★**
A great family-owned guesthouse. Good value.
*Calle de la Raccheta, Cannaregio.*
*Tel: (041) 241 39 35.*
*www.pontechiodo.it*
**Ca' Angeli ★★**
This B&B is wonderfully located on the top floor of the Grand Canal palace. Light, airy rooms and good services including a/c.
*Calle del Tragheto della Madoneta, San Polo 1434.*
*Tel: (041) 523 24 80.*
*www.caangeli.net*
**Hotel Adriatico ★★**
Conveniently located near the train station,

this is a comfortable, modern, yet modest small hotel which represents good value for Venice.

*Lista di Spagna, Cannaregio 224. Tel: (041) 715 176. www. venicehoteladriatico.com*

**Ca' Gottardi ★★★**

Ca' Gottardi is a mix between a B&B and a boutique hotel, with a great location and some rooms with canal views.

*Strada Nova, Cannaregio 2283. Tel: (041) 275 93 33. www.cagottardi.com*

**Casa Rezzonico ★★★**

A six-room B&B with an inner courtyard and some rooms with views of the canal.

*Fondamenta Gherardini, Dorsoduro 2813. Tel: (041) 277 06 53. www.casarezzonico.it*

**Hotel Antico Doge ★★★**

The romantic Palazzo del Doge Marin Falier has been restored with original antiques, hardwood floors and all mod cons.

*Campo SS. Apostoli, Cannaregio 5643. Tel: (041) 241 15 70. www.anticodoge.com*

**Pensione Accademia Villa Maravege ★★★**

This former residence and Russian Embassy is in a great location near the Grand Canal. Rare for Venice, it has lovely gardens.

*Fondamenta Bollani, Dorsoduro 1058. Tel: (041) 521 01 88. www. pensioneaccademia.it*

**Charming House DD724 ★★★★**

This contemporary boutique hotel is part of a new breed in Venice. It's modern and warm at the same time, with extensive facilities.

*Ramo da Mula, Dorsoduro 724. Tel: (041) 277 02 62. www. thecharminghouse.com*

**San Clemente Palace Hotel & Resort ★★★★**

Located on an island (San Clemente) in the lagoon, it's a luxurious five-star hotel with spacious rooms – something that's not easy to find in Venice itself – with tennis courts and a spa.

*Isola di San Clemente 1, San Marco. Tel: (041) 244 50 01. www.thi-hotels.com*

**Al Teatro ★★**

Located near the Fenice theatre, this friendly B&B has three spacious rooms; Verde, Ambra and Rosa. Wi-fi in the rooms.

*Fondamenta della Fenice, San Marco 2554. Tel: 333 918 24 94. www. bedandbreakfastalteatro.com*

## EATING OUT

**Alla Vedova ★**

Also known as Trattoria Ca' d'Oro, this authentic little place is worth seeking out for its *cicchetti* (appetisers) such as *polpette* (meatballs).

*Calle del Pistor, Cannaregio 3912. Tel: (041) 528 53 24.*

**Muro ★★**

A local favourite, this is a buzzy, fun and modern restaurant with great service, fine pizzas and a wonderful *ragù* Bolognese.

*Campiello dello Spezier, Santa Croce 2048. Tel: (041) 524 16 28.*

**Osteria Antico Dolo ★★**

While photos of famous visitors line the walls, it's not a celebrity hang-out but just a great, welcoming osteria.

*Ruga Rialto 778.*
*Tel: (041) 522 65 46.*

**Osteria Bancogiro** ★★

This osteria is at its best during the warmer months when you can sit outside and watch the canal traffic go by. Classic Venetian dishes.
*Campo San Giacometto,*
*San Polo 122.*
*Tel: (041) 523 20 61.*

**Alla Testiere** ★★

An informal and modest restaurant that has a well-cemented reputation for wonderful seafood dishes. It only holds a couple of dozen patrons, so book ahead.
*Calle del Mondo Novo,*
*Castello 5801.*
*Tel: (041) 522 72 20.*

**Ai Gondolieri** ★★★

This is a great local restaurant – one that locals visit when they eventually tire of seafood. It's not inexpensive though.
*Fondamenta*
*dell'Ospedaletto,*
*Dorsoduro 366.*
*Tel: (041) 528 63 96.*

**Da Fiore** ★★★

Allegedly one of the best restaurants in Venice, but apart from its fantastic front table (where you

can almost touch a gondola as it goes past), the food rarely rises above competent.
*Calle del Scaleter,*
*San Polo 2202.*
*Tel: (041) 721 308.*

**Osteria Anice**
**Stellato** ★★★

Try the mixed seafood as a starter at this family-owned restaurant.
*Fondamenta della Sensa,*
*Cannaregio 3272.*
*Tel: (041) 720 744.*

**ENTERTAINMENT**

**Teatro La Fenice**

Opera in Venice is held at this marvellous theatre. If you want to see an opera, it's best to book before you leave home – the website has details for buying tickets online.
*Campo San Fantin,*
*San Marco.*
*Tel: (041) 786 511.*
*www.teatrolafenice.it*

**Verona**

**ACCOMMODATION**

**Hotel Accademia** ★★★

This hotel is well positioned close to the Arena. Despite being a hotel since 1880, it is modern with a full range of amenities.

*Via Scala 12.*
*Tel: (045) 596 222.*
*www.accademiavr.it*

**Due Torri Hotel**
**Baglioni** ★★★★

Widely considered the best hotel in town, the standard ('classic') rooms are very small and it's only when you get to the suites that you'll feel like Mozart.
*Piazza S. Anastasia 4.*
*Tel: (045) 595 044.*
*www.baglionihotels.com*

**EATING OUT**

**Antica Osteria Al**
**Duomo** ★

A great little osteria serving up local dishes to a local crowd. The lack of tourists might be because of the donkey and horse on the menu.
*Via Duomo 7a.*
*Tel: (045) 800 45 05.*

**Osteria al Duca** ★

It's not the legend that this was Romeo's birthplace that keeps locals coming back to this convivial restaurant; it's the pasta and polenta (try it with gorgonzola).
*Arche Scaligere 2.*
*Tel: (045) 594 474.*

**La Bottega del Vino** ★★★

Serious food and serious wine. This is the best

place to try horse as the *Sfilacci di Cavallo* (horse meat with oil and lemon dressing) and *Pastissada de Caval* (stewed horse meat with polenta) are something special – as is the legendary wine list.
*Vicolo Scudo di Francia 3.*
*Tel: (045) 800 45 35.*

### ENTERTAINMENT
**Arena di Verona**
The main attraction in Verona, this arena is famous for its summer opera festival. Pop, rock and other concerts are held during the year as well. You can purchase tickets through the website.
*Piazza Bra. Tel: (045) 800 51 51. www.arena.it*

## Vicenza
### ACCOMMODATION
**Albergo Due Mori** ★
Centrally located, this is a great-value hotel which has a lovely feel, with 19th-century and Art Nouveau pieces scattered throughout the 30 rooms and public areas.
*Contrà Do Rode 24.*
*Tel: (0444) 321 886.*
*www.hotelduemori.com*

# TRENTINO-ALTO ADIGE
## Bolzano
### ACCOMMODATION
**Hotel Greif** ★★★
Close to the main square, this is a very stylish hotel with excellent facilities, friendly staff and parking.
*Piazza Walther.*
*Tel: (0471) 318 000.*
*www.greif.it*
**Luna-Mondschein** ★★★
An attractive and serene property which dates from 1798, rooms here have lovely mountain or garden views. The rooms are decorated in a typical local style and the hotel's restaurant, **Van Gogh**, is one of the best in town.
*Via Piave 15.*
*Tel: (0471) 975 642.*
*www.hotel-luna.it*
**Parkhotel Laurin** ★★★
A very comfortable, well-equipped hotel. Superior rooms (and above) are very generous in size. Great restaurant.
*Via Laurin 4.*
*Tel: (0471) 311 000.*
*www.laurin.it*

### EATING OUT
**Hopfen & Co** ★
Traditional inn with hearty fare and boutique

beer brewed on the premises.
*Obstplatz 17.*
*Tel: (0471) 300 788.*
*www.boznerbier.it*
**Torgglhaus** ★
A popular local pizzeria with hearty toppings that attracts skiers and hikers hungry after a day of serious calorie burning.
*Via Museo 2.*
*Tel: (0471) 978 109.*
**Wirtshaus Vögele** ★★
This traditional *Wirtshaus* (tavern or inn) serves Tyrolean favourites to a local crowd.
*Via Goethe 3.*
*Tel: (0471) 973 938.*
*www.voegele.it*
**Zur Kaiserkron** ★★★
This elegant restaurant was recently refurbished and is a stylish addition to the city's dining scene. Michelin-starred chef Norbert Niederkofler's cuisine here is traditional, but the cooking and presentation elevate it to great heights.
*Piazza della Mostra 37.*
*Tel: (0471) 303 233.*
*www.kaiserkron.it*

### SPORT AND LEISURE
The area surrounding Bolzano provides some

excellent walking opportunities, including the Bletterbach Walk and the Renon Walk. Visit the tourist office for details (*Piazza Walther 8. Tel: (0471) 307 000. www.bolzano-bozen.it. Open: Mon–Fri 9am–6pm, Sat 9am–noon*).

## Cortina d'Ampezzo
### ACCOMMODATION
**Hôtel de la Poste** ★★★
One of the institutions that makes Cortina what it is today, this hotel has had the same family management since before World War II. Even if you don't stay, have a drink on the terrace.
*Piazza Roma 14. Tel: (0436) 4271. www.delaposte.it*
**Miramonti Majestic** ★★★★
Despite it not being right in the centre of town, this hotel is part of the town's fabric, just like the Hôtel de la Poste. Great facilities.
*Via Peziè 103. Tel: (0436) 4201. Email: hmiramonti. cortina@dolomiti.org*

### EATING OUT
**La Tavernetta** ★★
A local favourite near the ice-skating rink, the food here is very hearty – perfect after a day's hiking or skiing. Winter dishes include *ravioli di cervo* (with venison – a local speciality).
*Via d. Stadio 27a/b. Tel: (0436) 867 494.*
**El Toula** ★★★
This converted 'barn' is a real destination restaurant (it's a short drive out of Cortina) and well worth the effort for the views and the fantastic fresh pastas. Book ahead.
*Località Ronco 123. Tel: (0436) 3339. www.toula.it/cortina*
**Ristorante Tivoli** ★★★★
Ristorante Tivoli is modern Italian at its best. A wonderful showcase of regional ingredients, from the handmade pasta to the local lamb, it's an unforgettable experience.
*Via Lacedel 34. Tel: (0436) 866 400. www.ristorantetivoli.it*

### SPORT AND LEISURE
**Snow sports & summer sports**
Skiing and snowboarding are popular here and the tuition is first class – it's a great place to either start or take your skiing and riding to the next level. **Scuola Sci Snowboard Cortina** (*www.scuolascicortina.com*) are the best people to take lessons with. For summer hiking and biking information visit the Dolomiti website (*www.dolomiti.org*).

## THE DOLOMITES
### Alta Badia
### ACCOMMODATION AND EATING OUT
The tourism organisation covering Corvara, Colfosco, La Val and Badia has a long list of superb mountain resorts, hotels, B&Bs and apartments to rent in the area, as well as information on restaurants and gastronomic itineraries. See *www.altabadia.org*

### SPORT AND LEISURE
The tourism offices produce a wide range of excellent information on skiing, snowboarding, walking, hiking and Alpine mountaineering, with very helpful and detailed maps and itineraries with distances

and durations. They can also organise private guides and excursions. See *www.altabadia.org* and *www.altabadiaguides.com*. You can purchase a ski pass that can cover you no matter where you want to go. Visit *www.dolomitisuperski.com* to best calculate the right pass for you.

## Merano

### ACCOMMODATION

**Vigilius ★★★**

This mountain resort at 1,500m (4,920ft), with arrival only by cable car, is stunning. Sleek and minimalist, it's perhaps the coolest place to unwind in Northern Italy. Its **Restaurant 1500** is wonderful.

*Vigiljoch Mountain, Lana.*
*Tel: (0473) 556 600.*
*www.vigilius.it*

**Palace Merano ★★★★**

Merano's most charming, if imposing, hotel is this old-world wonder, with extensive gardens and spacious rooms. The legendary Henry Chenot spa soothes the muscles of the fabulously weary.

*Via Cavour 2.*

*Tel: (0473) 271 000.*
*www.palace.it*

### EATING OUT

**Sissi ★★★**

Widely considered the best restaurant in town, Sissi turns out refined Tyrolean cuisine.

*Via Galilei 44.*
*Tel: (0473) 231 062.*

### SPORT AND LEISURE

Vigiljoch, accessible via cable car (*leaves every 15–30 min*), has some wonderful walks that are well signposted, and some good cross-country and limited downhill skiing in winter.

## Trento

### ACCOMMODATION

**Castel Pergine ★★**

This romantic 13th-century castle has rustic touches at every turn. The restaurant is highly regarded.

*Via al Castello 10, Pergine Valsugana.*
*Tel: (0461) 531 158.*
*www.castelpergine.it*

**Accademia ★★★**

This historic hotel and restaurant is located right in the centre of town. Comfortable rooms and

a decent restaurant.

*Vicolo Colico 4.*
*Tel. (0461) 233 600.*
*www.accademiahotel.it*

### EATING OUT

**Al Vò ★**

This simple *trattoria* is popular for a lunch of filling pastas. Good local wine list.

*Vicolo del Vò 11.*
*Tel: (0461) 985 374.*

**Chiesa ★★**

A modish restaurant near the castle, it serves up creative renditions of classic Northern staples such as risotto.

*Parco San Marco.*
*Tel: (0461) 238 766.*

**Le Due Spade ★★★**

This cosy restaurant specialises in great local dishes, especially fish, with some very creative touches. Book ahead.

*Via Don Arcangelo Rizzi 11. Tel: (0461) 234 343.*

**Scrigno del Duomo ★★★**

This cellar restaurant is a highly regarded eatery with great takes on regional cuisine and a bar. Excellent wine list.

*Piazza del Duomo 29.*
*Tel: (0461) 220 030. www.scrignodelduomo.com*

174

# Index

# Acknowledgements

Thomas Cook Publishing wishes to thank TERRY CARTER for the photographs in this book, to whom the copyright belongs, except for the following images:

PICTURES COLOUR LIBRARY 96, 100
WIKIMEDIA COMMONS 97 (Pavel Krok)

For CAMBRIDGE PUBLISHING MANAGEMENT LTD:
**Project editor:** Karen Beaulah
**Copy editor:** Diane Teillol
**Typesetter:** Paul Queripel
**Proofreader:** Jan McCann
**Indexer:** Karolin Thomas

## SEND YOUR THOUGHTS TO
## BOOKS@THOMASCOOK.COM

We're committed to providing the very best up-to-date information in our travel guides and constantly strive to make them as useful as they can be. You can help us to improve future editions by letting us have your feedback. If you've made a wonderful discovery on your travels that we don't already feature, if you'd like to inform us about recent changes to anything that we do include, or if you simply want to let us know your thoughts about this guidebook and how we can make it even better – we'd love to hear from you.

Send us ideas, discoveries and recommendations today and then look out for your valuable input in the next edition of this title.

Emails to the above address, or letters to Travellers Series Editor, Thomas Cook Publishing, PO Box 227, Coningsby Road, Peterborough PE3 8SB, UK.

Please don't forget to let us know which title your feedback refers to!